LIVING WITHOUT LIMITATIONS
MORE STORIES TO HEAL YOUR WORLD NOW

Compiled by Anita Sechesky

LWL PUBLISHING HOUSE
Brampton, Canada

LIVING WITHOUT LIMITATIONS
– More Stories to Heal Your World Now

Copyright © 2018 by LWL PUBLISHING HOUSE
A division of Anita Sechesky – Living Without Limitations Inc.

All rights reserved. No part of this publication may be reproduced, distributed or transmitted in any form or by any means, including photocopying, recording, or other electronic or mechanical methods, without prior written permission of the publisher, except in the case of brief quotations embodied in critical reviews and certain other noncommercial uses permitted by copyright law. For permission requests, write to the publisher, addressed "Attention: Permissions Coordinator," at the address below.

Anita Sechesky – Living Without Limitations Inc.
lwlclienthelp@gmail.com
www.lwlpublishinghouse.com

Publisher's Note: This book is the Black & White interior version of the Anniversary color publication *Living Without Limitations - More Stories to Heal Your World*. This a collection of personal experiences written at the discretion of each co-author. LWL PUBLISHING HOUSE uses American English spelling as its standard. Each co-author's word usage and sentence structure have remained unaltered as much as possible to retain the authenticity of each chapter.

Book Layout © 2018 LWL PUBLISHING HOUSE

LIVING WITHOUT LIMITATIONS
– More Stories to Heal Your World Now

Anita Sechesky – Living Without Limitations Inc.
ISBN 978-1-988867-05-2
ASIN 1-988867-05-2

Book Cover: Steve Sechesky & LWL PUBLISHING HOUSE
Inside Layout: LWL PUBLISHING HOUSE team

TABLE OF CONTENTS

LEGAL DISCLAIMER 1

FORETHOUGHT 3

WITH LOVE AND GRATITUDE 5

DEDICATION 11

INTRODUCTION 13

CHAPTER ONE 19
    MORE Healing for the Body – Anita Sechesky

CHAPTER TWO 25
    My Healing Journey from Fibromyalgia – Rebecca David

CHAPTER THREE 31
    I Am a Caregiver and Healing Is My Goal! – Anita Sechesky

WORDS OF ENCOURAGEMENT 37
    Brandie Muse

CHAPTER FOUR 39
    My Heart Is the Health of My Wealth – W.A. Reid Knox

CHAPTER FIVE 43
    How I Found Strength and Beauty from Brokenness – Kim Thomas

CHAPTER SIX 47
    No Limits: Living Beyond My Abilities – Sujit K. Reddy

WORDS OF ENCOURAGEMENT 51
    Brian Baulch

CHAPTER SEVEN 53
    I Was Finally Wrapped in the Arms of a Hug – Sandi Chomyn

CHAPTER EIGHT 57
In the Blink of an Eye, the World I Knew Changed – Tim Rahija

CHAPTER NINE 61
Lifting My Spirit out of the Depth of Despair – Jill Gjorgjievski

WORDS OF ENCOURAGEMENT 67
Brian vela Ntombela

CHAPTER TEN 69
How a Positive Mindset Helped Me Heal from Neck Cancer
– Sarah Dickinson Bailey

CHAPTER ELEVEN 75
MORE Healing for the Mind – Anita Sechesky

CHAPTER TWELVE 81
I Am a Soul Survivor: Healing from Depression and Self-Abuse
– Kaila Janes

WORDS OF ENCOURAGEMENT 85
Candace Hawkshaw

CHAPTER THIRTEEN 87
Yes, I Can Be Sweet as Chocolate – Anita Sechesky

CHAPTER FOURTEEN 91
I Was Only Sixteen but I Survived! – Brian Baulch

CHAPTER FIFTEEN 97
In Search of Healing – Afya Ashiki

WORDS OF ENCOURAGEMENT 101
Diana Alli D'Souza

CHAPTER SIXTEEN 103
Life's Energy Can Heal You – Christopher Fink

CHAPTER SEVENTEEN 107
My Relationship Was Red Flagged! – Olive Walters

CHAPTER EIGHTEEN 111
Faith Roots Can Heal Your Future – Koreen Bennett

WORDS OF ENCOURAGEMENT 117
Elizabeth Ann Pennington

CHAPTER NINETEEN 119
I Broke through the Wall of Doubt – Patrick Hayden

CHAPTER TWENTY 123
Releasing to Begin Healing – Luciel Greene

CHAPTER TWENTY-ONE 129
MORE Healing for the Spirit – Anita Sechesky

WORDS OF ENCOURAGEMENT 133
Mary Hilty

CHAPTER TWENTY-TWO 135
The Power of Words – Natalie Bélair

CHAPTER TWENTY-THREE 139
I Will Never Forget Her Last Words to Me – Anita Sechesky

CHAPTER TWENTY-FOUR 143
I Never Got a Chance to Say Goodbye – Valentina Gjorgjievski

WORDS OF ENCOURAGEMENT 149
Pat Campbell

CHAPTER TWENTY-FIVE 151
The Crossroads to My Healing – Gloria Delvecchio Callan

CHAPTER TWENTY-SIX 157
Break Through the Bullying – Nathaniel Sechesky

CHAPTER TWENTY-SEVEN 161
A Stumble along the Crooked Path: A Chapter from My "Book of Life"
– Satie Narain-Simon

WORDS OF ENCOURAGEMENT 167
Sujit K. Reddy

CHAPTER TWENTY-EIGHT 169
Healing My Spirit and Broken Wing – Elizabeth Ann Pennington

CHAPTER TWENTY-NINE 175
I Was Living on the Edge – Stacey Cargnelutti

CHAPTER THIRTY 181
I Was That Little Girl – Carol Metz Murray

WORDS OF ENCOURAGEMENT 187
Sandi Chomyn

CHAPTER THIRTY-ONE 189
Living in the Fullness of Your Purpose, Passion, and Power
– Kim Thomas

CHAPTER THIRTY-TWO 195
Forgiveness: A Vehicle for Self-Transformation & Healing
– Michelle Francis-Smith

CHAPTER THIRTY-THREE 199
Nourishing My Soul – Natalie Bélair

WORDS OF ENCOURAGEMENT 207
Sarah D. Bailey

CHAPTER THIRTY-FOUR 209
How We as Parents Can Connect with Our Daughters
– Sharon Ann Marie Stewart

CHAPTER THIRTY-FIVE 215
Grief to Grow Through – Stephanie Roy

CHAPTER THIRTY-SIX 219
Social Media: The Magic behind the Personal Branding Tools for Everyone
– Sujit K. Reddy

CHAPTER THIRTY-SEVEN 223
Inspiration Comes from Our History and Determines Our Future!
– Anita Sechesky

CHAPTER THIRTY-EIGHT 227
Embracing Your EQ and Weakened Areas – Anita Sechesky

AFTERTHOUGHT 233

LEGAL DISCLAIMER

The information and content contained within this book *Living Without Limitations - More Stories to Heal Your World Now* does not substitute any form of professional counsel such as a Psychologist, Physician, Life Coach, or Counselor. The contents and information provided does not constitute professional or legal advice in any way, shape, or form.

All chapters are written at th*e discret*ion of and with the full accountability of each writer. Anita Sechesky – Living Without Limitations Inc. or LWL PUBLISHING HOUSE is not liable or responsible for any of the specific details, descriptions of people, places or things, personal interpretations, stories and experiences contained within. The Publisher is not liable for any misrepresentations, false or unknown statements, actions, or judgments made by any of the contributors or their chapter contents in this book. Each contributor is responsible for their own submissions and have shared their stories in good faith to encourage others.

Any decisions you make and the outcomes thereof are entirely your own doing. Under no circumstances can you hold the Compiler, LWL PUBLISHING HOUSE, or "Anita Sechesky – Living Without Limitations Inc." liable for any actions that you take.

You agree not to hold the Compiler, LWL PUBLISHING HOUSE, or "Anita Sechesky – Living Without Limitations Inc." liable for any loss or expense incurred by you, as a result of materials, advice, coaching, or mentoring offered within.

The information offered in this book is intended to be general information with respect to general life issues. Information is offered in good faith; however, you are under no obligation to use this information.

Nothing contained in this book shall be considered legal, financial, or actuarial advice.

The author or Publisher assume no liability or responsibility to actual events or stories being portrayed.

It may introduce what a Life Coach, Counselor or Therapist may discuss with you at any given time during scheduled sessions. The advice contained herein is not meant to replace the Professional roles of a physician or any of these professions.

FORETHOUGHT

"When we know Love, fear has no value in our presence. There is no pressure to perform and mask our humanity. We can BE and when we BE, we can inspire others to BE."— E'yen A. Gardner

We all go through life hiding parts of our real selves behind masks, appearing to have it all together, to have perfect lives and to have no issues or problems. Very few see behind the mask and even fewer get to know the real you. By hiding our stories, our hurts, our disappointments, our losses and our pains, we hope people will accept and love the false image of who we reflect.

As a community leader, church Pastor and Director of an outreach centre, I have spent the last twenty-one years devoted to helping individuals, from all walks of life, find the courage to take off the mask and allow the light of truth to bring healing and wholeness in areas of emptiness and brokenness. Witnessing the affluent and underprivileged, the famous and unknown, young and the elderly all become liberated, empowered and set free from the wounds of their past has become my life's mission and my heart's passion.

It's not until we choose to remove the mask and reveal our real inner truth, in all its convoluted mess and confusion, that our pains and hurts truly lose their grip on us, and we are launched into our unique and powerful destinies. The moment we face and expose them in the light of God's unconditional love, is the moment we begin the process of liberating every part of our being.

Anita has assembled thirty-two courageous heroes who have gone through this journey of vulnerably revealing their stories. They have opened their wounds, cleaned them out and have received authentic and lasting change through the victory of healing. As a result, they have gone from despair to destiny, pain to power, hurt to hope and trauma to triumph.

I applaud Anita's vision to show the world that they are not alone in their stories, I applaud the inspirational figures behind these stories for bravely removing the masks, and I applaud you as you read these stories and hope you are encouraged to take your own personal journey to wholeness. The bible says, "You will know the truth and the truth will set you free." I pray you find the truth and from this day forward you remove your mask and live in freedom.

Pastor Tania Meikle

Co-Pastor & Co-founder of Kingdom House, Brampton, ON www.kingdomhouse.com

Co- founder & Director of The Impact Centre – Community Outreach Centre, Brampton, ON (905) 459-5422

Honours Bachelor of Science Degree – University of Toronto

Founder of Revive Women's Ministry, Brampton, ON

International Speaker

WITH LOVE AND GRATITUDE

In hindsight, I recall what a feat it was in compiling this book initially with no virtual leadership experience, organizational skills, or guidance of any kind, working with colleagues from around the world in time zones I had never connected with before. I had just completed my first anthology "Living Without Limitations – 30 Mentors to Rock Your World," originally published on December 13th, 2013 (and scheduled to be republished by my company this year) which was the first book I had successfully compiled…it seemed literally like hours before. I didn't even have time to celebrate this achievement by selling signed copies in that launch period other than when I attended social or networking events.

Suddenly it was time to start all over again with the intake process of book #2 "Living Without Limitations – 30 Stories to Heal Your World." I had a stringent timeline to meet which meant fulfilling all thirty co-author spots and not knowing that in the end, I would be contributing MORE chapters than I had initially planned for. How fitting that we are here now four years later to be exact and my own publishing company is producing the revised edition of this beautiful book. Just to be clear, I had no choice given the circumstances but to write those six additional chapters and this also meant registering myself as the co-author of those chapters to be published, or there wouldn't have been any book for my co-authors and myself come April 11th, 2014. Yes, indeed I was in shock and what do you do when it all hits you like this? Do you walk away? Do you get mad, angry, complain, cry, and let yourself become bitter in it all? I thank God for giving me the strength to endure the things I went through and am so grateful for the peace that carried me through it all. You see, it's fantastic as an author to share a little piece of your heart and give a beautiful message at the end of it all, but when you are faced with a situation where you have no choice but to find healing even if you may have never processed the emotions connected to some significant life experiences, you become raw once again and numb as if a part of your bare soul is exposed and that is precisely what it was: my soul and the emotions that I had to share with the whole world were forced to be revealed. I decided to embrace it for all that it was in the blurry busyness that proceeded the next few days to write and write without limitations in my heart and soul. You see, there was no other way for me to produce the real-life content for this book, now that I look back at those past events. God indeed had a plan, and he wanted me to release the things that were holding me back, so he could use it to heal others who were still living in their pain. I had no option but to trust in Him...and so I did.

And here we are, four years later and celebrating my five-year business anniversary along with the fourth year of LWL PUBLISHING HOUSE.

Besides working on my six additional chapters as the compiler for the original edition, I was still in the process of working with each co-author who needed support writing their chapters; there was no time extension provided as I often give my clients now. I can tell you from this past experience, I quickly learned that putting things off will eventually catch up with you. Great leadership requires you to be looking ahead at where your team is and how they are also managing their responsibilities – it will eventually become your headache if there is no direction for the individual members on your ship.

You can imagine my surprise when the realization hit me that so many things I held inside of me for so long were now going to have come into print because I had less than seven days to submit these chapters to the publisher. This was one of those defining moments for me as a fresh author, a leader, and new entrepreneur who had just thought of writing as a whimsical hobby, BUT I was taking part in something much more significant than myself. Plus, the added responsibility of actually seeing this book published and providing the substantial finances required to make it happen in less time than I had originally prepared for. Yes indeed, it was an epic adventure. You never know what you will discover along the way.

With the first edition of "Living Without Limitations – 30 Stories to Heal Your World" being my second major international book project, I had somewhat prepared myself and managed to stay calmer and more focused despite my obvious burnout that those close to me were fully aware of. During this experience, I was still working full-time hours as an RN in the hospital and nursing home, with my young family to care for. Yet, I did not allow myself to get so emotionally drained like I was after the release of book one. What

Compiled by Anita Sechesky

a triumph when it became an International Best-Seller in less than one day on the market.

Many people may think that writing a book is a piece of cake. I would have to agree with them especially if it is a single author publication. However, in an anthology, what many people fail to realize is that you must be open-minded, literally remove your safety net, and step out of your comfort zone as the main author and compiler. I had to assume the role of consultant, coach, editor, and advisor with approximately fifty-five people for both Living Without Limitations books. I have seen myself become venerable to expecting just about anything to happen. In doing an international project of this capacity, you will travel all the time zones in less than twenty-four hours. When you finally get to have that long soak in the tub, you know that you have finally accomplished your mission. Since those early years, I have discovered how emotional intelligence is key to surviving as an entrepreneur.

To this project, I want to give a generous and compassionate "Thank You" to each one of my talented and courageous co-authors who have not only shared their own stories but took my request to be as real and as raw as they could be, to the next level. Their experiences will not only bring tears to your eyes, they will expose your heart and soul to a place that you may never have realized existed in this reality. My desire has always been for you, our dear readers, to step into these accounts as if you were right there with them. As human beings, we each have a body, mind, and spirit. We are all connected by spirit. We all feel emotions and experience life around us. Let us help you to heal your world, as we have found healing in ours.

I would now like to take this opportunity to acknowledge some very special people in my world.

To Stephen, the love of my life: Thank you for believing in me and my quest to always accomplish greater things in life. Your love, support, and friendship have proven itself through all the trials and hardships we have walked through. Where many have parted ways forever, we realized that the strength of our bond because of the children we brought into this world was greater than the division that life's failures could throw at us. Love heals where words fail. I admire and respect you for your patience, and determination to always believe that the best was yet to come for us. I look forward to spending the rest of our lives together discovering the blessings that God has for us as a family. Look what God has done. I love you always and forever.

To Nathaniel: Thank you for being such an amazing son. I love you more and more each day. You make me so proud to be your mother. You are an intelligent, kind, loving and respectful young man. I adore your sense of humor and appreciate all your extraordinary gifts unfolding that God has blessed you with. Never give up on your dreams. You were a success from the day you were born. I believe in you. Love Mom.

To Sammy: Thank you, my darling son, for the joy that you bring to Mommy. I love your curiosity as a child, always fixing and taking things apart. You have the mind of a genius, and wisdom beyond your years. The world is unfolding before your very eyes. God has great plans for your life. Plans to give you a future of hope and happiness. Success is in every step that you take. I'm so proud to call you "My darling little boy." I believe in you. Love Mommy.

To my beautiful and loving Mother Jean Seergobin: Thank you for always encouraging me to see the beauty in the world around me. I have learned so much from you and am a better person because of you, mom. You are my best friend and hero in more ways than you can imagine. To my wise and distinguished Father, Jetty Seergobin: Thank you for showing me that you must believe in yourself and not worry about what others are doing. You have taught me so much, and I admire the wisdom you have and the gentle heart you have towards helping those less fortunate than yourself. Mom and Dad: You have always believed in me when others have not. Because of you both, I have never given up on what God's plans are for my life. I can do all things through Christ who strengthens me. You both have taught me this, and you have also inspired me to be a better person. I can now look past my fears, failures and the criticisms of others. I am so blessed to have you as my parents. I pray God's abundant and continuous blessings over you both. May the blessings of God surround you always. Amen. I love you so much, Mom and Dad.

To my brother Trevor Seergobin: Thank you for allowing me the room to grow professionally and chase after my dreams. Your continued support, encouragement, and praise make me think of you more like my big brother, but I'm so proud to call you my "Baby Brother." I pray God's blessings over you now and always. May God grant you desires of your heart. Thank you for being such a great uncle and brother-in-law, I am so thankful for the plans that God has for your life to prosper and bless you always.

For all the people who have been part of my life and supported my dreams and ambitions, thank you for being the wonderful friends, colleagues, and family that you are. I love and appreciate each one of you. Over the years, you have proven who you are, and for that I am grateful.

Once again, I would like to give an unusual appreciation to those who have caused me great pain through the circumstances that caused me the loss of my daughter, heartaches that have made me lose faith in people whom I thought would never hurt me so badly or betray me, disappointments that showed me how weak others can be, and that I should always turn my eyes upon Jesus and not people. It was because of you; I never gave up. Thank you for being who you are and challenging me to become a better person than I thought I ever could have been. Through all those dark days, I found the strength I never knew I had inside. I FORGIVE.

I can do all things through Christ who strengthens me. (Philippians 4:13 NKJV)

More Stories to Heal Your World Now

Compiled by Anita Sechesky

DEDICATION

This beautiful world was lovingly made for all of us to live a life without limitations.

God has given us the free will to choose how we will live it.

HAPPINESS to carry us through the darkness.

STRENGTH for the tough times that come unexpectedly.

GRACE to face anything in life with a confident assurance of succeeding.

COURAGE to overcome all things that try to overtake us.

LOVE to cover a multitude of things meant to damage or destroy us.

PEACE to fill the quietness when we allow our Faith to rise up boldly before us.

With all of God's blessings at our fingertips, we have been FREELY given a choice to choose the life we want to live. I choose MORE good things this world has and all of God's blessings from above.

I choose life MORE abundantly!

Anita Sechesky

More Stories to Heal Your World Now

INTRODUCTION

Reflecting on how this Book was created, based on my BIG vision in the summer of 2013 when I extended the invitation to my original co-authors for the *"Living Without Limitations"* books, each chapter was focused on individual experiences that are centered around finding the balance of mind, body, and spirit to live a productive and healthy life. Upon reflection of the whole concept of this particular book, I can see how much we as a society needed to hear the messages lovingly written by each contributing author.

Interestingly enough, the most common thing I kept hearing from each one of my co-authors was how much they agreed we live in a world of broken people that needed MORE hope and examples of how others have survived what they lived through and still managed to successfully carry on with their lives. They all desired to be part of this life-changing book sharing their voices to help bring healing on an International level. This same emotion still rings true for our newest authors in this beautiful revised edition.

It wasn't until after receiving the initial drafts of their chapters that was I able to comprehend the magnitude of healing that was actually taking place within my co-authors and those closest to them. It was then that I realized the title needed to reflect the real purpose based on the concept of this book series. In this revised edition you will also discover beautiful and empowering affirmations lovingly sprinkled throughout this book to lift your spirit as you read these heart-wrenching stories regardless if the situation was about an individual, family, business related, health, or generally life-focused.

The stories that I have collectively brought together are all "true life" stories. They are neither fiction nor are they embellished to make it a better read. Be warned that they are "Raw," written straight from the hearts of these beautiful souls. When I interviewed each one of my co-authors, I didn't know their history or what they had walked through on their journeys to get where they are today. My team and I consist of the most amazing people you can ever meet. We are honest and sincere professionals who have conquered our greatest fears and now want to help you with yours.

Many times, I was shocked and taken back in tears when reviewing how "gripping" their experiences really were. I found myself asking each collaborator, "Are you sure you want to share this?" The common response was, "Yes! I need to share this if only to help but one person." WOW! This book had taken on a whole new level that I myself did not expect. Be prepared as you are introduced to some of the most powerful life stories of what it is like to be "Broken in your Spirit" and learn how to find your healing when all hope has been stolen, lost, or destroyed.

This book is intended to bring awareness of how powerful the human spirit indeed is. It doesn't matter where someone comes from; there is still a connection to others elsewhere. It doesn't matter what profession someone specializes in; there is still a connection to all people worldwide. It doesn't matter what age a person is; there is still a connection to all generations. It doesn't matter what gender someone is; there is still a connection to both genders. It doesn't matter what level of education someone has; there is still a connection to those with varying degrees of wisdom and knowledge. And it doesn't matter what religion or faith someone has; there is still a connection to all other faiths. All this can be found and experienced in our beautiful and diverse world if one truly desires to find it.

This book is meant for you and anyone else who is living with a life experience that may be related to any of the chapters within. It will help those who have never realized how powerful the human spirit really is.

Many times, we do not give ourselves, or others, the credit or acknowledgment for what they have endured through hardships, heartaches, pain, trauma, or abuse.

My vision for this book is that the reader will enter through the pages and begin a powerful journey that will expose deep layers in one's life. There may be things that you have not spoken of or shared with anyone ever in your life. I encourage you, if you have had, or are going through, any of these experiences or worse, please seek out professional counsel, coaching, or guidance from your medical provider, church leaders, school officials, employer, or otherwise. Putting your pain aside will only hurt you and your loved ones more in the long run.

If you are like most people, at some point in your life, you must begin an inner journey of healing by releasing the painful memories within your heart and soul. It starts with acknowledgment, forgiveness, and then love for the life that you now have. These experiences might be buried so deep that you may not even realize they are still there. Opening your mind, will, and emotions to the following stories will allow you to explore these things in your very life that may prove to be therapeutic to where you are right now. Many times, we don't realize how our experiences affect everything in our decision-making process as we move forward in our journey.

I can sincerely say that after having a background of over twenty years in healthcare, working closely with individuals in various institutions such as Adult day care centers, nursing homes, and hospitals that I have often wondered about the brokenness that I observed in my patients' eyes. As health professionals, my colleagues and I carry out treatment routines based on physical assessments, medical diagnoses, and information collected or provided by our clients and their families. The main objective is to promote health and healing from a physical, mental, or emotional perspective. Unless it is something that requires medicating, many people go through life with broken hearts and spirits that a medical team cannot help with.

Over the years I have witnessed how many people have based their choices on either the things they want to avoid or the things they want more of in their lives. It is a proven fact that we are creatures of habit. If we are comfortable with something, we will continue doing it that way. If we are avoiding things, it can usually be traced back to the negative experiences we had in life.

As an ICF – Certified Professional Coach, I have helped many people overcome limiting beliefs placed on them by negative and often painful life experiences so that they can write their stories from a place of healing, courage, and strength. Not everyone has the willpower to develop a strong and positive mindset to help themselves overcome and allow healing in their lives.

From my own life experiences both personally and professionally, there have been times I had to make some major decisions and was faced with these very thoughts: "What if?" or "Why not?" The "What ifs?" were fear based and always lead to one place: *I don't want to feel that way again.* So, therefore, my choice was already made for me. The "Why not's?" stemmed from my sense of motivation and courage. I don't know how I found the strength. But one thing was for sure, I was not going to worry about the outcome because I was too focused on the objective and purpose of my dream or goals at that very moment.

Many times, without realizing it, in order to accomplish the things I did, I had to decide to be my hero no matter what others thought or how they acted towards me. I am quite aware of the fact that sometimes in life we face circumstances where the difference between accomplishing something of great significance in one's life is deciding at that very moment we are more than what we have experienced or what others thought of us. Not everyone in our lives may be a supporter, motivator, or even healer. There are many people who will not even think twice about discouraging and destroying the hopes, dreams, and goals of others. Sadly, it may be based on their issues of jealousy or worse because they have no hope within themselves, so how can they believe in anyone else?

Broken people will only produce brokenness. They will continue a cycle without realizing they are actively contributing and creating more hurt in the world. This is a natural response which may not even be their own fault; it is what has affected their very souls and only proves that inner healing has not taken place. Perceptions become distorted and narrow. The options in life become very limited because the "safest place" is often not exposing one's self to the criticism or opinions of others. When an individual is hurt, they may begin to start labeling themselves and live in a world they secretly create if they have been victimized or taken advantage of in any way. Evidence of emotional healing is a healthy perspective towards others and your outlook on life.

There is a connection in the human spirit that I have witnessed in my own life that no matter what one has faced, forgiveness, love, compassion, and empathy can bring healing to many.

YOU may be the very person that needs to have some inner healing take place today. My desire for you, our dear reader, is that you will choose to be open-minded and compassionate, not judgemental, in a state of offense, or negativity when you read these chapters written with great Love and compassion just for you.

Even though you may have never walked through anything close to what my co-authors and I have endured, as humans we all desire to be loved and accepted for who we are and still decided at some point of our journey that there was more to live for in this beautiful world.

When we look around, there is so much to be thankful for. Many of you may have walked through worse than we have. Just like you, we all have a dream, and together we can walk in hope, peace,

Compiled by Anita Sechesky

and unity to bring healing one person, one soul, and one life at a time. We are the hands and feet of God, and it's time to replace brokenness, despair and hurt with "Love," the gift of our Creator.

Let's do it! We as one family of humanity can heal this world even MORE as one. Let it begin now with you and me.

Your experience to be Published, Coached or Mentored by Anita will be none other than Life Changing!

Anita is the Brampton Chapter President of the Holistic Chamber of Commerce because she believes in supporting all entrepreneurs who work from a mind, body & spirit perspective. As a Registered Nurse with over twenty years in Health Care, she has worked with all age groups and diversities.

Anita was a Float RN, that specialized her training to work in the following areas: Surgical, Cardiology, Oncology, Nephrology, Pediatrics, Respirology, Palliative, and Gerontology. She has been a Charge Nurse and Team Leader in a variety of healthcare settings from Nursing homes and hospital floors with specialized areas. Now trained as a Trauma Nurse, she works on a casual basis in the ED of various hospitals throughout Southwestern Ontario.

Anita has excellent written, and communication skills is empathetic and goal-oriented. She is as an ICF - Certified Professional Coach, Publisher, Law of Attraction Practitioner, and soon-to-be Master of NLP Practitioner, as well as a #1 and multiple Best-Selling author.

She is a highly sought-after Book writing mentor branding 352 international best-selling authors in the last four years. The founder of Anita Sechesky – Living Without Limitations Inc. and the Publisher of LWL PUBLISHING HOUSE, which empowers, inspires, and motivates both authors and their readers alike to step into living their best lives possible. She hosts a variety of events, such as *Inspired to Write - Talk Radio*, Self-empowerment and writing workshops and webinars as well as Living Without Limitations Conferences.

Let's connect today!

To book a Discovery Session with Anita, please send an email. Alternatively, visit our website below.

Email: **lwlclienthelp@gmail.com**

Website: **www.lwlpublishinghouse.com**

YouTube Channel: **https://bit.ly/2JortaC**

Anita's Private Facebook group: LIVING WITHOUT LIMITATIONS LIFESTYLE **http://bit.ly/1TlsTSm**

LinkedIn: **https://ca.linkedin.com/in/asechesky**

Twitter: **https://twitter.com/nursie4u**

Instagram: **https://www.instagram.com/lwl_publishing_house/?hl=en**

Blog Talk Radio: **blogtalkradio.com/lwlinspiredtowrite-talkradio**

CHAPTER ONE

MORE Healing for the Body
by Anita Sechesky

The human body is the temporary home of the human spirit. It is also the central location where life actions and reactions take place. Our body is the most complex and unique life form that has ever existed. Yes, there is an amazing diversity of living things on this planet, but the human organism is at a pivotal place in comparison to all of the world's other creatures. It is a living machine where life is created. Every organ is intricately faceted together to create a masterpiece of divine workmanship! The systems within our bodies are so detail oriented that even the most skilled engineer cannot duplicate the blueprint to create another human being from the ground up. Each system within our bodies has its own functions and capabilities that when working synergistically, forms human life as we know it.

Like a well-oiled machine, the human body functions flawlessly when it is taken care of. It receives much joy and happiness through the ability to assimilate responses from the five senses: touch, taste, sight, hearing, and smell. Our greatest accomplishments in life are often attributed to the condition of our bodies. When we maintain the function and state of well-being, our bodies will perform at optimal levels. The human body is intricately and wonderfully managed by itself. Yes, it is self-maintained to a certain degree. We, as the owners and caretakers, must contribute our role and give the appropriate attention as required to regulate it. With proper care, rest, and nutrition, it will continue to perform at optimal levels of endurance for longevity.

As we age our bodies require increased maintenance to continue the activities of daily living. We need to give special attention to ourselves. Are we receiving enough fresh air, physical activity, rest, relaxation, water, and nutrients to stay healthy? We must be encouraged to perform physical activity in order to maintain our full independence, free of assistance or ailments. Each of our bodies was created with distinct characteristics that take on its own personality and reactions through our unique DNA. Many people go through their lives not giving a second thought to taking care of their bodies. Life can become so busy and responsibilities get in the way. Before you know, another day has ended, yet no effort has been made to stay healthy.

The great thing about this life though is that there's no better time like now to start doing the things you need to do. For instance, when was the last time you did the physical activities you know you should be doing? Sleep is one of the basic things that is required by everyone, but how much are you actually getting? When you sleep, that's the time your body effectively communicates within itself. The various organs, its systems, and complex cellular activities co-ordinate themselves to promote homeostasis, the act of creating balance within the body resulting in increased health and well-being. During the day, our minds are bombarded by so many actives and responsibilities to attend to. It is not until we shut down for the night that our bodies can be entirely communicating with our brains, which by this time has begun to sort out all the tasks of the previous day. Goals, setbacks, emotional outbursts, and unexpected events are just a few of the memories that must be processed to effectively achieve balance. By the time these are sorted out, our brains then begin to have direct communication to give all its energy and focus on what the maintenance chores are for your body. These include eliminating wastes and toxins, fuelling and repairing our cells, as well as processing the communication between the organs and systems. WOW! What a big job! Aren't you proud of yourself? You should be so pleased that you are healthy and on your way to daily healing.

Your mind, body, and spirit are a fantastic team that coordinate everything within your human entity to keep you alive! Please take care of it. You only have one body for life. Many people, knowingly or unknowingly, abuse their bodies without realizing the long-term harm or damage they are doing (although wear and tear naturally occur due to the everyday functions of life). We can still promote healing within our bodies by making the right choices now. We should begin to listen to what our bodies are trying to tell us and connect with the doctors and professionals who know the intricate details of our physical makeup. They can help us work even better and recover from losses due to environmental or physical damage. There are many modalities that can be used to assist us in this process, but one must be willing to seek out the care and attention with the right resources available.

Here are some of the simple ways we can promote healing within our bodies:

- Avoid processed foods, bad fats, and sugar-laden items.
- Exercise regularly.
- Get the rest you require.
- Limit your stress load.
- Visit your family doctor regularly for baseline health statuses.
- Research ways you can promote a healthy life for yourself.
- Spend quality time with loved ones.
- Love yourself more – your body knows!
- Do the things that challenge and increase your physical endurance if you have medical clearance.
- Do not self-medicate.
- Avoid substance abuse of all kinds.
- Take your prescribed meds as ordered by your doctor.
- Be aware of your physical limitations.
- Make informed decisions from reliable sources based on the best outcome always. Do your research and present it to your health provider.
- Take good care of your body. Don't stress it out!
- Don't be an emotional sponge. Let go of everyone else's issues.
- Practice forgiveness and release all of the negative energy.
- Visualize your body being at optimal levels of health.
- Associate with others who have healthy lifestyles.

- Pamper your body once in a while: bubble baths, Jacuzzi, massages, etc.

- Get involved in fun actives that stimulate your senses at the same time, such as Ballroom Dancing, Belly Dancing, sports, hobbies, etc.

- Take extra care with the kind of things you feed your body. Are they healing and promoting health?

- *Maintain an expectancy of hope.* Never give up when facing situations or circumstances.

As a Registered Nurse who has worked in many healthcare departments with people of all age groups and diverse physical ailments, I am aware that most people, including myself, depend on our health care system. However, my thoughts are that individuals should be encouraged to start allowing their bodies the chance to begin healing now before health issues arise. Give yourself the positive reinforcement *(HOPE)* it needs to feel good. The joy and happiness you can create with a positive mindset will get you further ahead in life than you can imagine. Who knows, it might even help to prevent many of life's ailments that can be directly related to stress-overload, not only from emotional burdens but also physical demands. We can help to control the load of stress on our bodies quite effortlessly by making informed choices when it comes to our food, environment, and relationships. How sad when people are sick or diagnosed with an illness by their doctor that possibly could have been prevented had they sought out the professional counsel and guidance earlier. I have often observed this in life because our society is so fast-paced, active, and constantly changing that many people don't give themselves the chance to allow their bodies the opportunities required to bring about basic health and healing. Do you know anyone who fits this picture?

Life is only as complicated as we allow or want it to be. Our bodies are just like any other machine. They will eventually burn out if they don't get the attention and upkeep that they deserve. If you are struggling with negative thoughts towards your health and life in general, ask yourself, "Why?" The society that we live in today provides so much information and guidance to help everyone achieve and maintain a standard of health. Seek out the counsel that you require. If you are still unsure what direction to go, discuss this with your health provider.

As you read through the chapters of this book, many of my

co-authors have struggled with their situations and life events. But they haven't given up. They found HOPE. Everybody deserves the chance to believe in their healing and well-being. You know that you're worth it. You are perfectly created in the image of your Creator. Allow yourself the privilege of letting go of all your fears, doubts, and heartaches. Nothing is impossible if you honestly believe. If it can happen for others, why can't it for you? After all, you are a valuable person. Everyone that knows you is blessed by the joy that you bring to this world.

Your body is the home that you have been given to live the life that you desire. Don't give up. Live your Life without Limitations. Give yourself the chance you have been waiting your whole life for. With a positive mindset, informed choices, and a hopeful attitude, you can begin a healing journey right now.

Anita Sechesky

Anita is the Brampton Chapter President of the Holistic Chamber of Commerce because she believes in supporting all entrepreneurs who work from a mind, body & spirit perspective. As a Registered Nurse with over twenty years in Health Care, she has worked with all age groups and diversities.

Anita has excellent written, and communication skills is empathetic and goal-oriented. She is as an ICF - Certified Professional Coach, Publisher, Law of Attraction Practitioner, and soon-to-be Master of NLP Practitioner, as well as a #1 and multiple Best-Selling author.

Email: **lwlclienthelp@gmail.com**

Website: **www.lwlpublishinghouse.com**

More Stories to Heal Your World Now

Compiled by Anita Sechesky

CHAPTER TWO

My Healing Journey from Fibromyalgia
by Rebecca David

My path to pursue a career as a holistic life coach came about through my own chronic illness and that of my loved ones; this chapter is about overcoming my own incurable illness of fibromyalgia.

At first, I thought I was experiencing some sort of flu or virus, but it was lingering far too long and the symptoms were increasing in duration and intensity. Suddenly I was having a hard time making it up the stairs without gasping for air; just doing laundry was exhausting! Shooting pain appeared throughout my body without warning and in random places! Soon I began to experience horrible headaches due to the intense pain in my neck and upper body. I clearly remember wondering what in the world was going on with me. I also thought I had something wrong with my heart because it was often beating rapidly and irregularly. I had frequent chest pain, intense fatigue, and pain everywhere! I had such difficulty breathing at times, especially with any exertion, when I tried to exercise I was unable to move without feeling that my bones were going to break! The intensity of the symptoms varied – sometimes on a daily basis, sometimes weekly – but it was not going away. I cried a lot because I really wanted to do so much and be more active with my family but I was so exhausted and in pain!

After many months of feeling this way I knew it was time to see the doctor. I felt nervous and was thinking it must be very serious to have something suddenly attack my body and disrupt my lifestyle as it was doing! After a full examination and lab work, to my surprise my medical tests were normal, the doctor said everything looked good! I left the visit feeling very confused and with a couple of prescriptions to treat the symptoms.

I sought out several specialists in hopes of receiving answers and solutions, but the only thing I received was a variety of drugs to treat the symptoms; anti-inflammatory, anti-depression, sleeping pills, muscle relaxers, anti-anxiety, etc. The drugs did not heal me nor did they take the pain away; however they did add to the exhaustion, mental fog, and loss of enthusiasm for daily life! It was such a frustrating time, to say the least. I was in a lot of pain, but when I took the medications I would often be so very tired or nauseous. Don't get me wrong, I was happy I didn't receive some serious medical diagnosis, but I was baffled how I could be in so much pain, yet it not be evident to the doctors.

A few years passed and the symptoms continued and even progressed. I had been to several doctors and came away from each visit with the same question in my mind, Are You Kidding Me? I felt they didn't take me seriously and that all I was experiencing was not valid to them. I actually considered going to the next doctor appointment wearing some scruffy clothes and without makeup just to appear disheveled in hopes they could somehow actually see the pain I was in and find answers for me! Sounds a little silly I know, but I felt so discouraged to continually hear how good I looked outwardly when I was living with so much pain.

My appointment with a new highly recommended rheumatologist began much like all the other doctor visits, he asked the same questions the other specialists asked. I was getting tired of saying the same story over and over again. After the exam and reviewing my lab tests he said it appeared I had fibromyalgia. He explained that there wasn't a lot known about this syndrome, but it was becoming more common, especially among active women my age. I left the office that day with more prescriptions to take but no hope for a cure.

Well as strange as it may sound, I honestly felt a sense of relief because there was a name for what I had. It was some sort of validation for all I had been experiencing. However, a feeling of hopelessness came over me on hearing there was nothing I could do to heal this pain and fatigue – and that it could very well get worse. Wow, what a range of emotions!

For a brief time, I accepted this incurable syndrome and my lot of living with it. Several of my family members also had Fibromyalgia and would say things like "It's in our family genes," or It's our fate."

That was very unsettling to me! Many months went by, and I started to feel depressed. This affected me on all levels because I couldn't find a way to heal it – my daily life and my daily joy were suffering.

After my primary care physician received the report of Fibromyalgia, she spoke with me on the importance of reducing stress in my life and getting good nutrition. I took her advice and began research and implementation of a regimen. There were so many times I felt exhausted but I continued to search out and implement different approaches. I started receiving massages, began journaling, focused much more on good nutrition, researched and used many therapeutic grade essential oils. I nourished my body, mind, and spirit with healthy choices and it really paid off! I am so grateful to say that through the holistic protocol I was following the intense pain and constant fatigue began to decrease, and over time it went away completely! I have been functioning at full capacity with zero Fibromyalgia symptoms for many years now; what a difference!

Writing this chapter has brought to memory a difficult time in my life but it is with gratitude that I share this with you to offer hope and encouragement to pursue your own healing, a healing that empowers you and brings about a greater sense of vibrancy in your life. In many ways, my healing journey from Fibromyalgia was a gift to me, a gift that allowed me to look at my life in a deeper way. I was carrying a lot of stress emotionally & physically and it manifested in my body.

Dear reader, if you have Fibromyalgia or any other debilitating health concern and are suffering, in pain and hurting, I encourage you to seek out answers, resources, and tools that will give you optimal health to enjoy life. You will see for yourself the positive changes taking place. It really is possible! There is an epidemic of syndromes and diseases that present with similar symptoms. Many of the traditional methods of treatment cause further problems, like my own increased fatigue, brain fog, upset stomach, etc. We are all different, what works for one may not work for another. There is so much that can be done to ease your daily pain and suffering, and there are a lot of resources available.

True healing takes place holistically, meaning an integrative approach to treating the entire person – body, mind, emotions, and spirit. It is a very personal journey; we are each different, and therefore your holistic protocol should be tailored specifically to you.

Here are a few ideas to consider as you begin your healing journey:

- Practice deep breathing frequently. It's a great way to relax, reduce tension, and relieve stress.

- Cultivate awareness. Become more aware of every aspect of your health; choose positive and healthy thoughts and nutrition.

- Improve your nutrition. Eat more fresh vegetables and fruits, avoid processed food as much as possible, increase healthy fats and drink at least half an ounce of water per pound of body weight.

- Research health and healing. There are many free resources on the Internet and at health stores.

- Hire a coach. Working with a holistic life coach can be very valuable; a coach can work in partnership with your physician to assure you are able to live a quality life. If you choose to partner with a coach, choose one who will work with you to create a holistic protocol designed specifically for you. A professionally trained life & health coach will help you process and balance the many emotions you may encounter and will empower you to continue moving forward.

- Embrace the healing journey. When you fully embrace all you are learning and going through, you will begin to understand and appreciate yourself at a much deeper level, providing an even greater opportunity to heal.

With sincerity from my heart, I encourage you to believe there is a healthier way to live, one that eases your pain and provides more energy, I hope you will pursue it diligently. This journey is a never-ending process, for there is always an opportunity to learn and grow. I am so grateful that I am on this healing path and I want to encourage you to begin your own healing journey today. Please don't give up, pursue with diligence your own recovery and healing, it is very much worth it! This is my personal story, I am not a doctor, please seek a health care professional for your health needs.

With much love & gratitude,

Rebecca

Compiled by Anita Sechesky

 Rebecca David is double certified as a Life Coach & Health Coach with extensive training in the Functional Medicine model of nutrition. She is a co-author in all three of the "Living Without Limitations" International Best-Selling books. Rebecca is passionate on empowering herself and others to change unwanted behaviors, overcome obstacles, reduce unhealthy stress, and live a healthy vibrant life full of gratitude and love.

Email: **Rebecca@rebeccadavid.com**

Facebook: **Facebook.com/ahealthyvibrantlife**

Facebook: **Facebook.com/rebeccasjoy**

More Stories to Heal Your World Now

Compiled by Anita Sechesky

CHAPTER THREE

I Am a Caregiver and Healing Is My Goal!
by Anita Sechesky

In 2007 my late aunt was diagnosed with lung cancer. It was devastating news for the entire family. My aunt was the older sister of my mom. As a family, we were coming to terms with this news and trying to be as supportive as we could be long distance. During that summer, things got worse. We learned that my mom had also been diagnosed with cancer. My second child was only a few months old. I was off on maternity leave from my nursing position at the hospital and was still breastfeeding him, so my days were full as my six-year-old son was now in school full-time.

At this time, we received news that my aunt was given less than six weeks to live. My mom made a very difficult decision, and as a family, we had to support her request to travel from Toronto to Vancouver. Because mom could not eat solid food, she was very weak and got tired easily. Although the flight was long and tedious with the commotion of airport travel, my mom endured it and was determined to see her big sister for the very last time. After we had arrived in Vancouver, I made appointments for mom with a Naturopathologist as she already had a specialist in Toronto and I wanted her to still receive medical care and be free from complications while away from home. Mom received the medical attention she needed while in Vancouver and always said how energized she felt after her treatments. I was so happy despite the circumstances. I made sure my mom was given the care she required that was available.

The Naturopathologist advised my mom to make an appointment with her doctor right away. It was scheduled when we arrived home and mom followed through with her appointments.

The reason I am sharing this story is because of the faith that we as a family had to create. This was new territory for us and we had never walked this path before. We lost my aunt on my mom's birthday, less than a week after we got back home. Even though it was expected, given my aunt's terminal diagnosis, as a family it was still a great loss for us all since my aunt was the glue that kept the family together. She always went out her way to be there for everyone and support their goals in life. Auntie made sure everyone in her family felt important and cared for.

Because my mom's appointments were right around the corner, there wasn't a lot of time to grieve. As her daughter, I realized how much she depended on me to help her stay strong through this whole ordeal. I prepared her meals and literally took care of her around the clock. I had no help and I still had my young family to look after, so it was a very trying time. What was hurtful was hearing that a few individuals were criticizing me for being irresponsible to my mom because I supported her decision to go to Vancouver to say farewell to her big sister.

One evening we had a visit from a minister. I distinctly remember the conversation getting heated as this individual had the nerve to challenge my mom's belief and faith about healing. I personally believe everyone has the right to form their own opinion when it comes to their life and what their desires are. When someone goes through a crisis, their faith is already being tested and challenged.

We were visiting my mom on the day she was admitted into the hospital as she was scheduled for major surgery the next morning. At that moment in my mom's life, what I observed that she needed was acceptance and support in her faith. This is what fuelled her will to survive. I recall there was an unpleasant conversation where I had to speak up. One individual who was visiting my mom in the hospital didn't give a second thought in regards to discussing about people who had already died. I was horrified. This was the last thing that needed to be in my mom's memory prior to going "under the knife," thinking about death and dead people. They were ignorant and disrespectful of her feelings and emotions at that moment. Even though I was upset and worried about the impact this would have on my mom, at my dad's request I apologized right away for being so outspoken, even though I felt it was not appropriate. Where were they when it came to my mom's care or best interest all along? I decided that was now their issue whether the apology was accepted or not.

As a nurse, I have great respect for the field of psychology and how the human brain translates conversations, emotions, and their effects upon all the systems of the body. I am a firm believer that positive reinforcement and faith goes a lot further to help promote homeostasis or healing, which can also be called harmony within the cells. Intelligence is a key factor in understanding our diverse and complex biological makeup. When going through a crisis in life, our brain uses all of its memories, emotions, and knowledge to fuel the "Will to survive." We become what we feed our mind. My goal for my mom was to maintain a calm and peaceful state of mind going into a surgery where she had to put her complete trust and faith not only in God her Creator and Heavenly Father, but also in the medical team at the hospital in Toronto. I already knew that she was struggling to stay positive for us, her family. But I wanted to make sure that she was not giving up either, especially with this trauma being only two weeks after the loss of her dear sister who was like a mother to her.

On the morning of my mom's surgery, my mom's younger sister, my dad, and my brother met me and my husband and our two children at 6 am. We as a family held hands and prayed. The surgeon was Middle-Eastern and respected our prayers. In fact, he even allowed me to pray over him and bless his hands. That was a blessing that helped to increase our faith as a family.

I learned through my mom's eighteen-hour surgery, recovery, and then six weeks of grueling radiation treatments that determination and willpower coupled with love for her family and faith brought my little four-foot eleven mom through living hell. I have so much admiration and respect for my mom. She is completely cancer free and a living testament to what faith, forgiveness, and loving others despite their negative attitudes can accomplish in one's life.

For those of you walking this journey beside your loved one, who may be going through pain and suffering, I want to encourage you that the world needs more human angels like yourself. Sometimes the burden is too great to bear for those we care for. As a care provider, you will endure many long days and nights. There may be times that you feel burnt out and weary. The life that you are used to may be long forgotten. Just remember that your loved one needs you now and it may be the difference between them giving up on their own life altogether. Stay positive! Bring joy wherever you go. Refresh yourself! Whatever you do, know that your love and dedication is not wasted. Indeed, there may even be times that you feel unappreciated or rejected. Others may not understand, but at the end of the day, you will have peace knowing that you never gave up and your love and support is exactly what the Great Physician ordered.

For those of you walking your journey alone, either by choice or not, I want you to know that God does love you and that you are not alone. You are important and valuable to everyone around you. Believe that your life has a purpose and if you haven't found it, what are you waiting for? Don't give up. God has a plan for your life. Do you have one for yours? Every positive action that you take will result in an equal and positive reaction.

What you focus on becomes your reality. Do you want more love? Then give it to others. The simple things we do end up being the most valuable to others. Healing begins within your heart. Learn to love yourself again. Allow others into your world. Seek out support systems in your community, church, school, or place of employment.

As human beings, sickness is not a foreign thing. Unfortunately, it may strike at the least convenient times in one's life. Many are not always fortunate to have the love and support of their family and close friends. No one ever said that life was easy. From the day we are born, it is a struggle to survive. We depend on others to clothe us, feed us, and clean us. Then we slowly learn through the following years how to do these things for ourselves. Our lifecycles revolve from being dependent to independent and then if sickness strikes before aging, we become dependant on others all over again. One thing is sure; we've all been given this one chance to make the best of this life we have.

Anita Sechesky

Compiled by Anita Sechesky

Anita is the Brampton Chapter President of the Holistic Chamber of Commerce because she believes in supporting all entrepreneurs who work from a mind, body & spirit perspective. As a Registered Nurse with over twenty years in Health Care, she has worked with all age groups and diversities.

Anita has excellent written, and communication skills is empathetic and goal-oriented. She is as an ICF - Certified Professional Coach, Publisher, Law of Attraction Practitioner, and soon-to-be Master of NLP Practitioner, as well as a #1 and multiple Best-Selling author.

Email: **lwlclienthelp@gmail.com**

Website: **www.lwlpublishinghouse.com**

More Stories to Heal Your World Now

WORDS OF ENCOURAGEMENT

I've had many obstacles to overcome considering I'm affected by Cerebral Palsy. But nothing I've experienced compares to the challenge of becoming a published author. Finally, I achieved that long-term goal.

So, if you have the will, there will be a way to achieve whatever you want in life.

BRANDIE MUSE

More Stories to Heal Your World Now

Compiled by Anita Sechesky

CHAPTER FOUR

My Heart Is the Health of My Wealth
by W.A. Reid Knox

The tower controller at Martin State Airport, in Baltimore, Maryland ordered, "You are cleared to land Mooney November Two Two Two Eight Kilo (N2228K), Instrument ILS approach runway 15 and watch for traffic...should be Medevac State Police Trooper Two leaving from the Helipad." My instructor told me that we were going to keep practicing these instrument-only approaches all day until I could hit the landing threshold every time! Flying was so much fun and such a challenge for me, and I miss it every day. I had the best flight instructor – who even flew with me from the east coast to the west coast just for the fun and the experience!

Flying saved my life and almost took it several times over the years. Let me explain how flying saved my life. Every so often your pilot's license needs to be renewed. Well, it is the medical examination part of the process that took away my license to fly.

I went to the Aero Medical Examination appointment with expectations of breezing right through, as I was in great shape and running five miles a day. However, the doctor looked up from listening to my heart and said, "Did your doctor ever tell you that you have a heart murmur? You need to see a cardiologist before I can clear you to fly again!"

Those words would be echoing in my ears all week, as I waited to see my friend and fellow squash player and now my cardiologist. He first listened to my heart and then sent me across the hall to have an echocardiogram. The operator of the machine which was imaging my heart and measuring all aspects of each beat says, "Son you have the heart of an eighty-five-year-old man. There is a huge calcium deposit in your aortic valve, and you will need surgery (I was a healthy middle-aged man, I thought). I am not supposed to tell you any of this, so act surprised when the doctor tells you!"

The doctor told me I would, in fact, need surgery, and I almost passed out in his office. I had never had that feeling of disbelief, raw fear, and dread before in my life. I then heard him ask me if I wanted a dead person's valve, a cow valve, pig valve, or mechanical valve? I clearly had some homework to do and many more medical tests, and I managed to put off my surgery for several years as my condition, a bicuspid aortic valve with a large aneurysm, was closely monitored for changes. As the aortic aneurysm reached the critical threshold in size where surgical intervention is recommended, I was forced to decide what kind of valve I would get, and I chose an On-X with New Mechanical Aortic Heart Valve which was very new at the time and not recommended by my cardiologist or surgeon. The implantation of my valve was to be the second one implanted at the hospital by a world renowned surgeon and his amazing team.

The process of preparing for a life-threatening surgery is different for everyone, but for me, the thought of dying or being crippled from the surgery was so scary, and I felt just fine the way I was. I was thinking, "Why am I deciding to do this to myself? Am I making the right choice with a mechanical valve? Is this the right doctor? Is this the right hospital?" Suffice it to say that a million questions went through my head every day until I found myself saying goodbye to my wonderful wife and five children. Then I was wheeled into the operating room to have my life change forever. I remember very little about what happened next, but when I regained consciousness I was strapped down on a gurney with a tube down my throat and a mechanical respirator breathing for me.

I remember I could see a clock and it was ticking; I remember the nurse telling me to be still and stop thrashing and fighting the machines that were keeping me alive. I heard the doctors and nurses running down a checklist of items, kind of like one I would go through before flying my plane – only this one was used to save a person's life. The patient in the bed next to mine was crashing, and they re-opened her and were trying everything they could to save her, but she died. I then remember being moved to a new location and listening to the nurses arguing with each other as they wheeled me and my machines to another location.

When I finally had the tube removed from my throat, I was so happy to be alive and really wanted a sip of water or an ice chip! To my surprise, I was too weak even to lift a paper cup. That was how much this surgery had taken out of me. I had just survived the procedure of "total circulatory arrest," where my body was cooled to about 64°F by a heart-lung machine, and my head and chest and body were packed in ice. My heart was stopped, lungs deflated, and all the blood was drained from my body into the heart-lung machine. I was clinically dead. The heart-lung machine was turned back on after the surgeon finished replacing my aortic root with a Dacron graft and the On-X with New Mechanical Aortic Heart Valve and reattached the major arteries to the graft. A patient can survive in this state for about forty minutes before the process damages the brain, heart, or the lungs. My entire procedure was somewhere around eight hours long, and I was one of the luckiest people in the world that day, and it was Friday the 13th of June, 2008.

I remained in the cardiac intensive care unit for the next seven days, waiting as patiently as I could to get a permanent pacemaker implanted. I had wires and tubes coming out of everywhere, and a temporary pacemaker that was run by replaceable batteries was sitting in my lap keeping me alive. Every so often my cardiologist would come in and turn it off to see whether my heart would beat on its own again. I would just about lose consciousness each time; it was like being in Oz. Sometimes the electrical pathway of the heart is damaged in the surgery, and the bottom of the heart doesn't get the electrical message from the top of the heart that it is time to beat. I gradually had to accept that I was in the "1% of people" that this happens to. At least this was a complication that could be fixed. I now am kept alive by a small computer implanted below my collarbone, and I am a grateful walking miracle of modern medicine.

Your Health Really is Your Wealth

Without your health, it really doesn't matter how much money you have, what your job is, where you live, or anything else like that. When I faced a surgery of this magnitude, looking death in the face, what mattered the most to me in my life was my family. My amazing wife, my mother, my four daughters, and my son were there to help take care of me at the hospital and during my recovery at home. My brothers and sister were there for me on the phone as well. If anyone out there reading this has any doubt about how amazing and wonderful this was, let me assure you that having my family care enough about me to be there for me when I really needed help was the greatest gift I have received in my lifetime. I am truly the most grateful person for the gifts of love and family that have been bestowed on me.

For anyone that is going through any heart disease and needs to have a heart surgery believe me that I get that "THIS IS GOING TO BE JUST A ROUTINE PROCEDURE" is something we all hear from our doctors and our friends and family. Believe me when I tell you that it doesn't feel that way when it is YOU who is going on the operating table. Now that I have recovered, I can tell you that I have never felt better than today, having just survived past the critical five-year anniversary of my surgery. Although I am no longer a private pilot, there are many other fun things that I can do every day, especially being a father.

There is hope and health beyond the surgery, but courage and valor and fear and death are in between...and LOVE is what cured me! That is just a small part of my story; May God Bless You Too!! I encourage anyone that can relate to my story, or if you would like to work with me around any fears you may have and how it is affecting your business or life, I am a Professional Life and Business Coach and am available at the following links below.

W. A. Read Knox is an International Best-Selling Author and Certified Life Coach living in Hunt Valley, Maryland, USA. He is the father of five children and has one grandchild. Read is a Realtor and has experience in numerous businesses over the years involving Aviation, Trucking, Mortgage Banking, Natural Health, Professional Sports, Frozen Foods, a licensed Life and Health Insurance and Investment Broker. Read is an avid athlete with a passion for Squash, Tennis, Skiing, Motorcycling, Polo, Hockey, Sailing, and Traveling. He wrote the chapter "Break The Blocks to Business Success!" as a co-author in *Living Without Limitations – 30 Mentors to Rock your World*.

Email: **Readknox@gmail.com**

Facebook: **facebook.com/read.knox**

Website: **www.readknok.nerium.com**

Website: **www.awesomewater.info**

Compiled by Anita Sechesky

CHAPTER FIVE

How I Found Strength and Beauty from Brokenness
by Kim Thomas

I would have never anticipated my fate on that sunny and crisp fall day on October 19, 1987 – also known as Black Monday – when stock markets around the world crashed. Well not only did the financial markets crash that day, but so did the vehicle I was driving in on my way to the dentist with my younger brother. I was seventeen at the time, and while that seems like a lifetime ago, it is very clear to me that the lessons I learned from that near-fatal car accident would set in motion many things that would help shape my life today. It fueled my lifelong passion to help others realize that there is something greater inside us that enables us to overcome every adversity, and that strength, beauty, and courage truly come from within.

My car had been hit by an erratic driver who was going over 100 mph, blazing through the red light and hitting my car broadside, sending it airborne. The car was crushed and witnesses couldn't believe we were still alive. Thankfully, my brother hadn't sustained any life-threatening injuries – but even today those gripping moments that we shared still give us an unshakable bond.

The first to arrive at the hospital was my mother. Doctors warned her, "Your daughter's entire body has been badly broken." But their dismal report did not intimidate her; instead, she fought fear with prayer and unshakeable faith. My brokenness extended far beyond my physical trauma. Inside I felt helpless. I saw my future flash before me; every dream faded as I lay there with many questions of whether I would ever walk, see, or even look the same again. I had many head injuries including a fractured skull, a detached eye, shattered facial bones, deep lacerations on my face, a broken collarbone and a shattered humerus. And over 70% percent of my blood was depleted, causing the most imminent fear of death.

At seventeen, I didn't understand that God would allow us to become broken in order to build us up. The doctor who performed the eye surgery warned my parents that while he was able to re-attach my eye, it was unlikely that it would function normally again. Another doctor warned that while I would walk again, there were no guarantees that I would have full mobility. The plastic surgeon said he could eventually bring my face back, but couldn't guarantee what normal would look like. What a dismal report, but thank God for my close-knit family. My mom, dad, and three brothers rallied by my side to speak words of life. My brother, who is now a Pastor, read Psalm 23 to me every day. Yet I still struggled with the feeling of despair. I couldn't see past my present circumstance and couldn't help but feel bitter because I should be at school training for track & field, rehearsing for the school play, getting ready for Grad photos or getting glammed up to attend Prom like everyone else. I just wanted to enjoy the things that typical teenagers do. Instead, I was worried about what my future would look like.

There were days when I felt like I was at my own funeral; visitors often looked mortified when they came to visit. One of my friends even threw a vase of flowers at the window in a rage, sending shattered glass everywhere, prompting nurses and security to rush to this scene of fury. Because my face was stitched and wrapped shut, I wasn't able to comfort my friends and reassure them that I would be alright, but truth be told, I myself wasn't convinced that I was going to be alright. After several angry and loud visits, security was posted outside of my room and eventually, my elderly roommate requested to be moved – the mayhem was becoming too much for her.

The next morning, I asked the nurse if she could wheel myself over to the washroom so I could see myself in the mirror. Strangely, she said that strict orders had been given that I wasn't to see myself, because I was on suicide watch. Did they really think I would kill myself? Now I was really curious about what I looked like, so the next day I asked my mom to bring in a hand mirror, so I could finally look at myself. With no hesitation, my mom said, "Of course I'll let you see yourself because one day you will look more beautiful than ever." In that still and quiet moment, my mom placed the mirror in front of my face with such confidence, but to my greatest fear, what I saw was more horrific than I ever imagined.

Part of my hair shaved off, the rest still knotted together with blood, a disfigured nose, a bruised and stitched up face, and even worse, my face was so big and swollen that it couldn't even fit in the mirror! At that moment I was so angry with my mom for even suggesting that one day I would look better. Overcome by despair, I asked God why He hadn't just allowed me to die. I realize that people go through tragic circumstances all the time, but no one ever expects that tragedy will knock on their door.

After feeling that I had hit rock bottom emotionally, I decided that I was going to fight the good fight with faith. I pulled on something that was greater than me. The Words of hope and healing began to manifest not only in my mind and spirit, but also in my physical body. Though still weak, I began to feel strong. I soon realized that no matter how much someone prays for you, ultimately, you have to believe it for yourself. You have to trust that all things are possible and that when you have no words at all, simply having faith the size of a mustard seed is enough to move mountains.

I quickly realized that God was on my side and was waiting for me to unleash that giant called faith that He deposits in all of us, but which only we have the power to activate. Although I was in a lot of pain, looked horrific and was uncertain of my future, I was grateful to be alive and realized that He that is within me, is greater than any circumstance. I said, "Lord use me to transform other lives through this experience." At that moment, I could hear God audibly say, "I saved you because I have great plans for you. Do not fear because I will take care of you and give you a future and a hope."

Fast forward to several months later, I began to see miracle after miracle in my life. Doctors were blown away. Even though I experienced much transformation, it took some time before I really felt and looked normal. I often fought back tears and faked confidence, yet I could hear a still small voice reminding me, "When you are weak, I will make you strong." I moved forward, knowing that my destiny and calling were greater than my insecurity.

Two years after the accident, I was miraculously healed and didn't even require the plastic surgery that was scheduled for me. They say everything happens for a reason, and I totally believe that. This trial has allowed me to speak to countless people over the years, especially girls that struggle with low self-worth. It birthed my mantra that strength and beauty come from within and that we are born to make a difference. It is time to see every test as a triumph, every battle as a blessing, and every opposition as an opportunity.

Our life has purpose. One that we often ignore and don't fully walk in. Let your difficulties fuel your faith and become opportunities for God to catapult you to higher heights – so when you rise from the valley to the mountaintop, you have greater vision, passion, and purpose. Know that every adversity you face is an opportunity for God to unleash His power.

You only know how strong you are when you are faced with a battle, but there is something greater inside of you that builds character, perseverance, and compassion. There's redemption lying deep within that brokenness. Make room for God and allow yourself to embrace every struggle and circumstance because there's purpose on the other side of that pain.

Through life's experiences, you quickly learn that when you have nothing but faith, that's all that you need. When adversity comes your way, don't take it personally, take it spiritually. The mantle of greatness doesn't come easy. We all have to fight through battles to get there, but God beckons to us to be still and know that He is God. Find hope in the detours that life brings, because your miracle is someone else's miracle. Believe, trust and have faith like your life depends on it.

Kim Thomas is a Lifestyle Architect dedicated to helping people move forward in life. Her devotion is to serve, inspire, and encourage. Her mission is to help others achieve personal mastery and transformation. Kim is a speaker, Life and Wellness coach, workshop facilitator and founder of onLIFESTYLEwithkim. A teacher and success coach over twenty years, her extensive background with youth at risk and in the arts as department head, creative director, actor, writer and producer have given her a well-rounded platform. Kim's mantra is to give back to the world more than we take. She is the mother of three extraordinary kids. All glory goes to God.

Facebook: **Kim Thomas**

Instagram: **Kimnthomas**

LinkedIn: **Kimnthomas@gmail.com**

Compiled by Anita Sechesky

CHAPTER SIX

No Limits: Living Beyond My Abilities
by Sujit K. Reddy

Let me start from the beginning so that you get a clear sense of who I am and where I have come from. I was born on February 25, 1977, in Toronto, Canada. I was the first-born of two loving immigrant parents from India. I have two loving younger sisters.

I was born with spina bifida and hydrocephalus. Being born with the medical diagnosis of spina bifida meant my spine was deformed at birth, and as a result, I am not able to stand or walk, nor will I ever in my life. So, to move about, I use a manual wheelchair. The medical diagnosis of hydrocephalus at birth meant I was born with too much water on the brain. This excess water was drained in an emergency surgery, by way of implanting a shunt which is a long thin tube that unraveled inside of me as I grew. The shunt starts at the back of my head and drains into my abdomen. Fortunately, this shunt has never been a serious medical concern in my life. As a side effect, I do have a few slight learning disabilities to do with math and writing; but over the years, I have figured out ways to manage them.

I have had many struggles, trials, and tribulations throughout my life, as we all do. I was not raised by my parents to use my physical challenges and the few limitations that come with them to have people feel bad for me, take pity on me, or most importantly, feel sorry for me. I was raised by my parents to be an equal in my family and the world. I have two younger sisters and growing up, if they were rewarded for something good they did, I was rewarded in the same manner. On the other hand, if they were scolded for something bad they did, I was scolded for the same thing, in the same way.

My parents instilled in me that I must show the world that, although I am in a wheelchair, I am able to live beyond it. In other words, to focus on the positives in everything that life hands you. Even my given birth name "Sujith Kumar" is a constant reminder of this, as it translates from Sanskrit to English to mean "Victorious Prince," which I have always taken to mean that I should never give up, no matter what!

I feel it is important to make specific mention of my father. He passed away when I was just seventeen. My father was not only my father but my best friend and first mentor. He taught me how to live and be independent. Looking back on the time that I did have with him, I have come to realize that he taught me – both directly and indirectly – everything I needed to know in life.

I will give you some examples to illustrate this. Both will come from the numerous family vacations we took together. My father directly taught me how to manage in any situation and any surroundings. For instance, there would always be a different setup regarding washroom facilities, whether it was in the hotel room or if we were staying with relatives or friends. My father taught me to adapt and change based on what was available to me in each case and not to focus on what was not. Indirectly, my father taught me how to deal with people's reactions to me and who I am as a human being. Whether it was looks, stares, glares or comments, my father taught me how to react in a positive manner to such negativity.

As a result of my childhood travel experiences, I have always enjoyed traveling to various destinations in the world as an adult. Such places have included various states of the United States of America and different countries in Europe and Asia. Throughout my travels outside North America, I have noticed one theme. That is, people with disabilities aren't always treated as equals by their respective families, communities, and societies. What I have observed is that people with disabilities are often "forgotten" and "put aside." Infrastructure and attitudes are not supportive to allow a person with any form of disability to live freely and independently as it is in North America for the most part. Every time I have traveled, I feel so blessed for the life I have had and the opportunities I have been afforded living in Canada.

I have traveled to India numerous times, as the majority of my extended family resides there. For those of you who have not been there, India is not known to be the most accommodating or accessible country in the world. I must say though, in the past twenty years, India has made some effort towards being more "livable" for all persons with disabilities. This is mostly due to foreign investment, but it still has a long way to go as a nation to equal the standard of living that people with disabilities experience in North America. I will give you an example from a sightseeing tour of Northern India that I took with my family and cousin.

One of the main stops on the tour was the world-renowned Taj Mahal in Agra, India. This was something on my "Live List" that I had always wanted to do. It has been declared an "historic" site. As a result, no accommodations have been made to make it accessible. If you have ever had the opportunity to visit the Taj Mahal, you will know that the stairs, to get up into the main courtyard, are steep and narrow. I took one look at the gentleman who was "assigned" by the tourist administration, to "help" me up the stairs, and knew I was going to be in some serious trouble if I were to get him to assist me. He was a frail man, in his 60s at best! He and his colleagues were suggesting it was too dangerous to get me up the stairs. I looked at my mom, sisters, and cousin and they instinctively knew what was coming. I climbed out of my wheelchair and pulled myself up the stairs on my own! I then had my sisters and cousin bring up my wheelchair behind me so I could use it around the grounds. There was no way, after traveling all that way that anyone was going to keep me from seeing this great Wonder of the World!

It is my hope that something I have said resonates with you, and I have moved you positively towards attaining your goals and dreams. I hope you have found something in what you have just read, to be and do better in your lives and fill the world with positivity, and let it shine and flow to those around you and even beyond that, to the entire world.

My entire life, I have always wanted to prove to the world that being a person born with a disability and in a wheelchair does not mean that life has to be limiting. I have made my life fulfilling and continue to do so every day.

As a result of the motivation and focus my parents have gifted me with, I have accomplished more in my thirty-six years than most "able-bodied" persons have and do in that same period of time.

Many parents of children with disabilities allow their child to coast through life and "take it easy," not allowing them to apply themselves, to change the world for the better. My parents never allowed for this to take place, and I am so thankful for that now because I am truly living life to its fullest, with a feeling of joy and abundance.

I have lived independently for over a decade now, with some assistance of government-funded attendant care (i.e., cooking, housekeeping, laundry) and have a decent and very active social life. You too can have the life you desire if you focus on the positives in your life!

"You can accomplish anything you put your mind to. Your mind ONLY has the limitations that you allow it to have.

Every person, regardless of the unique characteristics that make them who they are as an individual, has the right to live their life without limitations.

Do not let diagnoses or disabilities limit your potential as a human being. You were created for a purpose. Think BIGGER. Think past the confines of your limitations. Let healing begin within your life. Let go of all the labels and listen to your heart. Everyone can make a difference, one person at a time. Be courteous and respectful. Everyone deserves respect.

Sujit K. Reddy excels at everything his sets his mind to. He is a seasoned HR Professional who has had more than a decade of experience in influential roles that include working with three Canadian Financial Institutions (i.e., RBC, TD, and Scotiabank). Sujit runs his own HR consulting firm known as Human Capital Solutions. He is a seasoned speaker whose various topics use life experiences for all types of audiences. Sujit enjoys spending his free time traveling locally and internationally. Throughout his life, he has sought to make the world a better place.

Website: **www.sujitspeaks.com**

Email: **bookings@sujitspeaks.com**

Facebook: **facebook.com/THESujitK.Reddy**

Twitter: **twitter.com/SujitSpeaks**

Compiled by Anita Sechesky

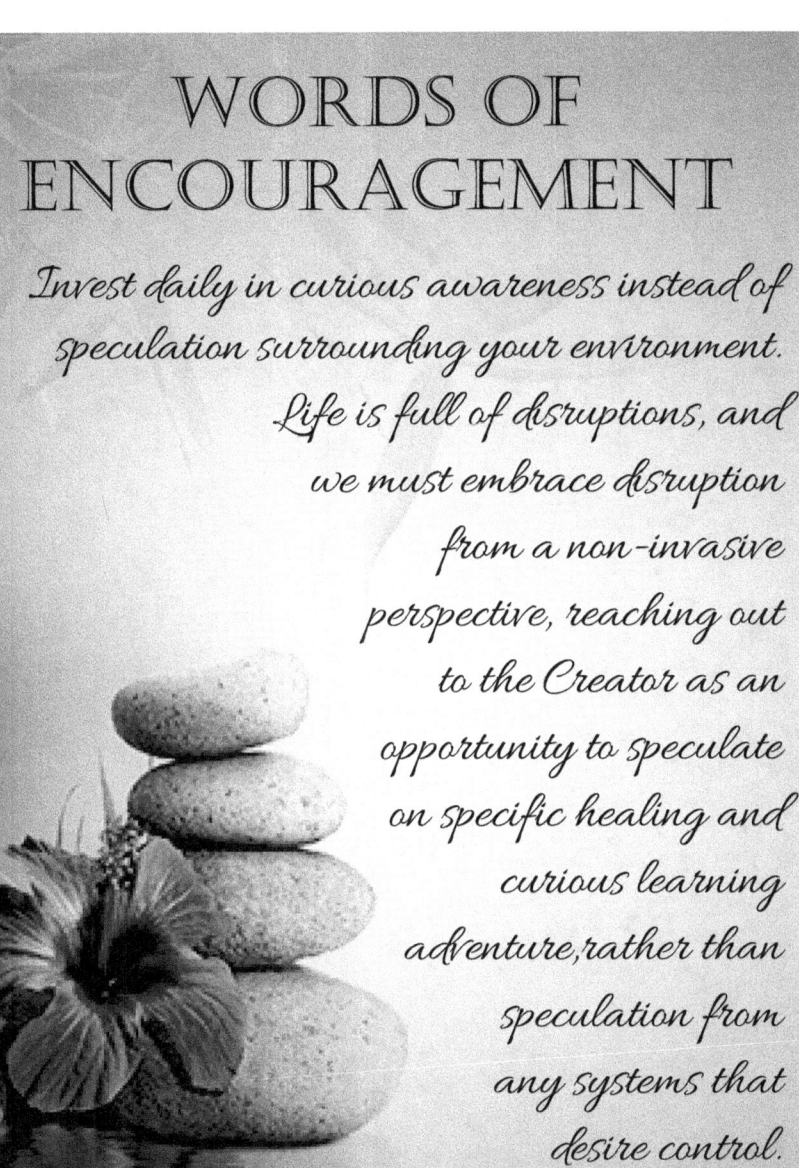

WORDS OF ENCOURAGEMENT

Invest daily in curious awareness instead of speculation surrounding your environment. Life is full of disruptions, and we must embrace disruption from a non-invasive perspective, reaching out to the Creator as an opportunity to speculate on specific healing and curious learning adventure, rather than speculation from any systems that desire control.

BRIAN BAULCH

Compiled by Anita Sechesky

CHAPTER SEVEN

I Was Finally Wrapped in the Arms of a Hug
by Sandi Chomyn

I was in a foster home from the time I was an infant. Looking back, there was a mixture of good and bad experiences.

Up to the age of seven, I did not realize or know I was in foster care until I was told I was moving to a new home and new people that would be looking after me. It was just me moving on, nobody else. Suddenly, I had the sense of uncertainty and confusion. I felt very scared and alone for the first time in my life. It made me think I had done them wrong and they did not want me anymore. I was the bad child.

This new foster mom showed me all of the things she thought and felt I needed to know about household chores. I learned about cleaning, cooking, laundry, and gardening and was given an education. She told me these were things I needed to know when I was older and would be on my own in the world. I was there until I got married. At the time it was an escape to get away, as I felt I couldn't make it on my own.

As long as I can remember from an early age, things were always very impersonal in both foster homes. Not knowing any different at the time, I thought it was normal. Even though I saw things were different in other people's lives, I did not question it.

At a young age did I realize I was learning about different emotions? In my own way, I most likely did but did not recognize them the same as others may have or should have or could have. My classmates called me retarded and teased me about being a foster child. I was always told by my foster parents and teachers that I would not amount to much of anything, because in their eyes they assumed I did not care or was a difficult child and student. In response, I felt like nobody cared about me. I felt I was never good enough in their eyes. I was doing, so I thought, all of the right things or the things they were teaching me to do, but I still felt that they were judging me. Even though I had done everything that I was supposed to do and was told to do. This made it more difficult for me to understand what was going on in my life. This, in turn, made me defiant as I felt that is what they wanted.

As I was getting older, I was starting to recognize things within myself with mixed feelings. There were many emotions I had that totally confused me. I started comparing myself to others and noticed that I was "different," and my perception of what I felt was normal was starting to make me ask questions. But the questions were only in my own mind, as I felt I should not or could not talk about it. And in reality, at the time, I felt I had no one to turn to.

It was important to know what was happening in my life. I needed and wanted someone to explain the situation to me in a way that I could understand, someone I could trust and talk to about things. But I never had that, and then just pulled away in many ways.

In my late teens, I was assigned a new social worker. When she came for scheduled visits, she took time with me. Suddenly, my opinions were important to someone. There were times she even asked me for advice. It was the very first time in my life that anyone seemed interested in me and my opinion. It helped me to start feeling confident in myself and to see that I had important things to share. She understood my needs, abilities, and capabilities. We worked together on my school work, and together we built up my self-esteem. I started to be proud of who I was and know I was a beautiful person. The relationship with my social worker provided me with stability and helped me to feel less afraid. I didn't change overnight. It was and still is an ongoing growth. Now I love to communicate and share advice as a life coach. Maybe that social worker is reading this right now. I would like to say thank you as I did not get a chance back then. She had moved on to new things in her life.

My biggest turning point was a lesson learned from my fiancé's mother. I had gone to the city with my future husband to go shopping and to the summer fair for the day. We then went over to his parents' house for the evening meal and for a visit. As we were getting ready to leave and chatting at the door my fiancé's mom reached out and gave him a big hug. As I was standing there waiting to go she turned to me and enveloped me in a big hug that had me in shock. I had never been hugged like that before. I stood there not knowing how to act or feel about it. Yes, I had had boyfriend hugs but never a hug from anyone else.

My fiancé's mom felt there was something missing when I didn't return the hug the same way she had given it. She looked at her son and asked what was wrong in her native tongue. Her son wasn't sure what to say. They both looked at me for an answer, which I wasn't sure I could give them.

Without saying much as it was an awkward situation, we let it go. I didn't though. I did a lot of thinking about it the next few days and weeks. I had a lot of mixed feelings about it because I wasn't someone who would talk about it, I internally processed it.

Days and weeks passed and I was to visit my fiancé's parents again. I still felt intimidated and unsure. We had our visit and were getting ready to go. Standing at the door my fiancé's parents gave him his hugs and "I love you." I was standing there waiting. When they were done; instead of them reaching out to me, I reached out and gave both of his parents a hug. I thanked my fiancé's mother for teaching me something special that day of the fair. I then explained to them that I didn't receive hugs growing up and that it was something new for me. She asked me why I had never been hugged. I told her what I only knew. I mentioned that I was a foster child and that they never showed the emotion to me like they did to their own children. Saying to her, somehow in my mind I thought it was normal but down deep knew it wasn't normal to even think the way I did. She said, "That was so wrong." We talked more about it through the years. For opening up to her, I was wrapped in the arms of a hug by my fiancé's mother. This was the start of many more hugs and "I love yous" to come.

My fiancé, at the time, also taught me someone did care about me and that I was more than good enough in their eyes. He always told me I am capable of doing anything I want and being the person I want to be. Through his love and understanding and not judging me, I have become that person. I have taught my own children that these two things are very important. They do not leave without receiving and giving hugs and saying, "I love you." All phone calls are ended with "I love you." Yes, I do work at it continuously. I am very happy to say I have been now been married for over forty years and now have an endless supply of hugs!!

After reading these experiences, there may be things that you may have wished were different in your life. You can have it. Things can be overcome and changed. A lot you probably have had to learn on your own, even how to show different emotions in many ways.

So many foster children go through life wishing for more and accepting just enough. Being complacent in the existence you have because of how you feel.

You have the choice and the power to make a difference in your life. A life coach can and will work with you. You tell your coach the topic and tell them what you would like to accomplish. Your life coach will work with you to come up with a plan on how to make your changes happen. Your coach will help you set up some accountability markers to ensure the success of your plan. Your coach will always be there for you along your journey. I can be that coach.

Sandi Chomyn is a Life Coach known as a Life Management Coach. After raising her three boys, she received her training from the Academy of Coaching Cognition. She's a farm mom and grandma, inside and out, and has come to enjoy the different facets of her life by integrating her life coaching business and her love for scenic photography with good country living. She's also an International Best-Selling Author with a chapter in the book *Living Without Limitations – 30 Mentors to Rock Your World*. She resides with her husband Bill in the small farming community of Togo, Saskatchewan, Canada

Compiled by Anita Sechesky

CHAPTER EIGHT

In the Blink of an Eye, the World I Knew Changed
by Tim Rahija

In June 2010, I moved to Texas to begin a new career in aviation. I was on top of the world. I had finally reached a major career goal after working extremely hard for the previous two years and was now working for a top company in aviation. I was very happy and proud of what I had accomplished and was thrilled to be doing what I had once dreamed of. I thought life couldn't get any better.

On Sunday, September 5, 2010, I had been out on my motorcycle and had been out with some friends that evening, enjoying a holiday weekend. I remember parting company and stopping by the store on the way home with the plan of spending the rest of a fun evening enjoying some quiet time. I was on my way home when, in the blink of an eye, my life took a drastic, major unexpected turn. The next thing I remember was waking up in ICU in Temple, Texas, with a tube down my throat, vision in my right eye significantly impaired and partially taped shut, my right leg in a cast from the knee down, and numerous lacerations and stitches in my hands and arms.

Right before waking up, I remember being in what felt like a dream state, and a vagueness of feeling myself on the ground, it was dark, and someone was trying to talk to me, asking me questions and me trying to answer that person. The next part was hearing a noisy commotion around me and being in an ambulance and the feeling of struggling to breathe, and a bright light above me with an EMT leaning over me and in a forceful voice saying, "Stay with me, Tim, stay with me," and the sound of the siren in the background. The next thing I remember was awakening to the sound of someone praying out loud for me and to see my dad and one of my co-workers at the foot of my bed. My initial reaction was nothing short of heart pounding panic. I was in excruciating pain, had a tube down my throat and couldn't speak, and I could barely see. I could tell I was in the hospital but had no clue of how I got there. Obviously, something very drastic and traumatic had happened. My Dad told me that I had been struck by a vehicle and a moment later was lying in the intersection with a shattered right orbit, broken nose, broken jaw and numerous other facial fractures, cuts, lacerations, six broken ribs, a punctured lung, and compound fractures in my right foot. I was transported to a local hospital for emergency surgery and stabilization and then flown to Temple because it has a level one trauma center.

Needless to say, it was a shock to the system to learn what had happened as I had no memory of being struck – and I still don't to this day. I had no idea of the true extent of my injuries, but I was alive and I thanked God for that simple fact. What was obviously crystal clear was that I was here by the grace of God for a reason, even though I had no idea why. I had no idea of what else there was to come. I knew that I was in more pain than I had ever experienced in my entire life. I was going to have at least two more surgeries; one for facial reconstruction and the other for my foot. I told myself that I had two choices; "You can ask 'Why me, why do I deserve this?' and be mired in self-pity and wonder how this is going to affect your career and the rest of your life. OR simply accept what has happened and harness the power you know is within you and figure out a way to move forward, get healed, return to work and get on with your life."

I remember thinking the choice was simple and obvious. I had been through tough times and circumstances before, but I had NEVER given up. I CHOSE to accept the situation because of my faith in God and belief that things happen according to his plan and that if God brings us to it, he will bring us through it. I chose to take ownership of my circumstances and make them my own and do something positive, as giving up and quitting was NOT an option. Nor was I going to allow myself to feel a need to "get even" with or judge the individual that made a critical error in judgment and almost killed me. I was going to refuse to be consumed with negative energy and thus refuse to give away my power. Additionally, I didn't have pessimistic or negative thinking people to influence my thinking or decisions, which was a blessing.

It was here that I took a big negative and turned it into a huge positive by tapping into the vast, unlimited potential within. After getting out of the hospital, I got back in contact with a co-worker who had shared a business opportunity with me prior to the accident and got my own business going. I decided I was not going to let anything hold me back physically or psychologically.

Here are the primary points I want to share with and impress upon everyone. I had no control over the injuries I had sustained or the lack of mobility. But, what I DID have control over was how I chose to respond to those events. I will tell you from experience that you can do whatever YOU decide and choose upon. Nothing can keep you from achieving whatever you desire unless you allow it. I'm human just like anyone else, and if I was able to take a painful, negative, and traumatic experience and turn it into an enormous, positive experience that allowed me to make significant personal growth and learn so much more about myself and serve as an inspiration to others, then so can YOU. I had gone from being perhaps just a few heartbeats from death, unable to walk and in constant pain management, to walking without assistance by early December, then returning to work without restriction by mid-January 2011. I even bought a new motorcycle a few months later. That is the power of mindset, faith, and belief in a nutshell. What you focus on is what you create and determines your reality. My advice to all is to refuse to allow life's challenges stop you from achieving. Confront those challenges head-on and strongly envision yourself demolishing them. Your subconscious will make it happen.

I want to take these same principles and apply them to what we do in every aspect of life and what our "Why" is. We all encounter difficulties in life. Do NOT let those become an excuse to give up and quit, just because the road gets bumpy. Change your thoughts and you change your life. Maintain passion and laser beam focus and resolve. Remember that nothing of value comes easy or quick. Life is a marathon, not a sprint. The key is to get clear life vision and purpose, develop a plan and strategy, establish a pace and work that plan. The ONLY person, who has the power to defeat you is YOU.

Here are some other things that I have learned and want to share. Ask yourself what is stopping you from getting what you want? Who YOU are always determines what YOU get. Is there something that you do or don't do consistently on a daily basis that has been stopping you from having and living the life that you know deep down you deserve and God wants for you? God did NOT create you for a life of mediocrity. What habit or habits stand in your way? Could it be things like fear, procrastination, complacency, pride or ego? What mindsets and beliefs do you have that are adopted from parents, peers, friends or others as a result of conditioning or programming that don't serve you? What color are the lenses through which you see the world? What beliefs do you possess that are holding you back?

Take a serious, but honest personal inventory of these things within and make a plan for change. If you can't figure any of this out and come up with answers, then you may be in denial. Truly effective, successful people can identify what they need to change to make themselves more effective. This process is called self-awareness. When you truly become self-aware, the obvious changes needed are revealed to you. Don't limit your challenges; challenge your limits. And, if at any time you feel you need special help along the way, do what I did and simply ask God. He is the constant support, especially in difficult times.

Tim Rahija is an aspiring entrepreneur, International Author, and business consultant with prior professional experience in Law Enforcement, United States Army, Human Resource Management, Information Technology, and Aviation Maintenance. He is Founder/CEO of his mobile application development company, Dreamscape Mobile Technology, started in 2012. He has been involved in additional business ventures in other technology platforms along with life coaching and personal development, based on personal life altering experiences, challenges, studies and training. Tim earned a B.A. in Human Resource Management from Mid America Nazarene College in 1989, and graduated summa cum laude from DeVry University with a B.Sc. in Information Technology in 2004.

Website: **www.21st-century-mobile.com**

Tumblr: **www.appreneur2013.tumblr.com**

Email: **timothy.rahija@gmail.com**

Facebook: **facebook.com/timrahija**

Twitter: **@MobileAppIncome**

Pinterest: **pinterest.com/timrahija**

Compiled by Anita Sechesky

CHAPTER NINE

Lifting My Spirit out of the Depth of Despair
by Jill Gjorgjievski

If you're like many women, chances are you go to great lengths not to burden those around you. I was no different, but the signs of stroke demand immediate attention, even if it seems like the worst possible timing.

I remember the night I experienced symptoms of my stroke like it was yesterday. I was sitting at my kitchen table looking out into the darkness, recalling the events of the day. I had just buried my husband and soul mate. I started getting hot, began sweating. I had chest tightness as if my heart was in a vise.

I had never felt so scared and anxious at the same time in my life. I was acting like I was completely ignorant of what was taking place. When my vision began to blur and I was unable to hold my cup of coffee, I told myself that it was normal to close up and not to feel anything.

My brain started to scream at me and I saw inside my head the sign "Alarm" in neon lights. "You are having a stroke." I said to my conscience, "No! I'm not! I'm just feeling numb – what do you expect? I just buried my best friend – the only person in the world I could talk to and trust." Feeling sorry for myself I continued to stare out the window my body stiff and rigid, trying to keep some control of myself. Then I heard a soft voice outside of my head that whispered in my right ear, "You are having a stroke Jill, but it will be alright if you allow us to help you." At that point my nursing instincts took control and I realized I had nothing in the house that would help if I was actually having a stroke. My brain still screaming for me to take something for the stroke, I mentally answered the voice, "Ok so help me." The voice told me to relax and allow myself to slide to the floor. I did this, but before I allowed myself to slide down to the floor I took some over the counter medication to help relax me. The rest I don't remember.

I was awakened like from a sleep by the soft voice telling me to slowly get up and sit back in the chair. At first, I didn't realize what had just happened. I felt fine on the floor like I had a good night's sleep but as I went to get up my head throbbed like I had been drinking, my legs felt weak, and I could not stand up. It was a struggle, as my arms felt weak as well. Feeling like I had a hangover I thought to myself, "Well that medication had a good punch to it," while smiling to myself; but in fact, I was weak because of the stroke. I went to pick up my cup only to have it slide through my hands; I had no feeling from the wrist down. At this point, I started to panic a little, self-sabotaging thoughts like, "You're for the scrap heap now, no one is going to want you, and all the hard work was for nothing," crept in. I realized that I had lost the will to live and didn't care what happened to me. Although the spirit within me was screaming at me, giving me instructions on how to overcome this, I refused to listen.

In the days that followed, I did my best to hide my symptoms from my children, but they noticed that I couldn't hold anything or eat anything, which made them question me. They tried to convince me to go to the doctor, but I did not listen. I was too busy being stubborn and thinking what would happen if I was properly diagnosed as having a stroke. They had, without my knowledge, gone to the family doctor on my behalf but I would not budge. My eldest daughter then tried speaking to close family friends to come and speak to me in order for me to seek help.

Crunch time came or – if you like – a wakeup call, when one day my daughter came home all excited that she had bought me hair color and exclaimed that it was pamper night and she was going to pamper me and color my hair. I got angry and stated to her that coloring my hair was superficial and pointless since I felt worthless. She was determined; she responded back at me, "Please mum, I don't want you to be like the old widowed ladies. I want my classy mum back."

Her words penetrated the wall of stubbornness I had put up for protection, and for days afterwards her words played in my head. I realized that I needed to dig deep and find my inner strength again, if not for myself, for my children. This spurred me on to dig deep into my feelings and find the fighting spirit within me again.

Together with my children's support and my guardian angels by my side guiding me, I started on the path that led me back to health. For the next three months, this became a daily routine of healing. With each healing session, I had to dig deep and have faith that I would be able to find my inner spirit again to, fight the physical and emotional limitations I was experiencing, trusting that all would be well. At times this was not easy for me to do; I became overwhelmed to the point of being stifled and stuck as I peeled the layers of emotions that are associated with the loss of a loved one and surviving a stroke. With determination and a fighting spirit, I slowly regained feelings in my hands, my vision became clearer, my swallowing improved, and I was no longer choking on anything. My facial droop took longer to heal, but there was improvement and within three months I was well enough to get back to my normal routine with the business.

Dig Yourself out of your own Despair:

Whatever life gives you, even if it hurts, be strong and act like the way you always do. Because strong walls shake but never collapse. Obstacles don't have to stop you! If you run into a wall, don't turn around and give up. Figure out how to climb it, go through it or work around it. Find that one thing that will reignite your inner spark – that one thing that is your driving force – and focus on it as you go through your challenge.

In our physical experience, it is important to take the time to develop our emotions. The thoughts we use to create our reality are shaded by the emotional participation of our consciousness. Always attempt to align your emotional responses with actions rather than reaction. This way the participation is fully created from your core rather than another's.

Recognize the power emotions emanate whether they are positive or negative. Letting them run rampant is not a good use of the energy.

Learning to balance them within will lead to a better-created reality. Always remember that the beauty you have will radiate and shine through you in many ways, to touch the hearts and souls of many. You are the beautiful creature that is surviving in this world of madness; knowing that you can survive and hold a smile on your face, and love in your heart is one thing that you are to be grateful for. However, there are many things to be grateful for. It's about honoring the self within you, the courage within your being and finding the strength to face each day when times are tough.

You are a gift to yourself and you are the present that needs to be opened daily. But with that, it is allowing the heart to be opened to that you may fear, by those who may hurt you and step into that space of vulnerability. For you are the savior to your own graces, you are the bandage to your own wound, you are the beat to your own heart and you are the song to your own dance.

An emotional component exists in all of us. It is for you to decide how much to let it show. Know, however, that it does exist in every one of us. Engage it, Act within it. Become a more colorful creator; a full spectrum is available, however, you should decide to use it. It can be volatile, but in that energy, quite remarkable.

Take that step into beyond and know that you have the support and love of the Divine Spirit and know that you will always be blessed. Just allow and be the brightness that you choose to be in this world.

Signs of a stroke demand immediate attention, even if it seems like the worst possible timing or possible environmental side effects. Seek medical attention immediately; call your local emergency service at the first signs of stroke.

The information offered in this chapter is intended to be general information based on my own experience and general life issues. Information is offered in good faith; however, you are under no obligation to use this information. It is not meant to replace professional medical advice.

Jill Gjorgjievski is a Multi-Dimensional Healer/Teacher, Registered Nurse, Early Childhood Teacher, Certified Intuitive Life Coach, and International Author. She is a Master in Angelic Reiki, Unicorn Healing Energy, Faery Reiki, with the power of Love Energy Healing and she teaches these modalities. Jill is the founding CEO / Director of Gjorgjievski Enterprises, with the power of Love, Chocolates, and Things. Her vision and mission in life is to help people achieve balance and success in life using the highest vibration of love.

Website: **www.jgjorgjievski.com**

Website: **www.jillgjorgjievski.com**

Website: **www.withthepoweroflove.com**

Skype: **Jill.Gjorgjievski**

Email: **jgjorgjievski@yahoo.com.au**

Facebook: **facebook/jillgjorgjievski**

Google+: **plus.google.com/102253108963879351612/about**

Compiled by Anita Sechesky

WORDS OF ENCOURAGEMENT

Being faithful to yourself will lead others to be faithful to you, and together you will have faith in everything you do.

BRIAN VELA NTOMBELA

Compiled by Anita Sechesky

CHAPTER TEN

How a Positive Mindset Helped Me Heal from Neck Cancer

by Sarah Dickinson Bailey

"Focus on the health you want, not the illness you don't!"~Sarah d. Bailey

On December 3, 2012, when my surgeon uttered the words "We found cancer," a few things went through my mind. I was still a little groggy from the anesthesia. After all, I was still in the recovery room from what was supposed to be a simple surgery to remove a harmless cyst in my neck, but the doctors at Yale Medical Center found tumor cells in one of my lymph nodes. Before surgery, I had MRI and CT scans and biopsies, and they were all negative, so needless to say, I was at the same time shocked, confused and upset upon hearing this news.

I know the news of cancer is devastating to many people. Had I found out about it weeks before surgery, I might have been a little more freaked out about it, but I didn't have time for that. I barely had enough time to process the information before we were planning the next phase of treatment, which was to do six weeks of daily radiation treatments. I refused to do chemotherapy because I just didn't want to have those toxins in my body, but also, with the type of cancer I had, going through chemo wouldn't have improved my outcome much at all.

I never asked myself, "Why me?" because, I learned many years ago to ask instead, "Why not me?" I mean, what makes me so special that nothing bad should ever happen to me? An even better question is, "What can I learn from this experience?" or "How can I be refined during this process?"

Since I know a little bit about the power of the mind, I decided almost immediately that I wasn't going to let cancer become my identity. I took the attitude that I was going to conquer cancer. I realized that the treatments and the side effects were going to be painful, but it was just something I had to get through. There's way too much for me still to do on this earth to be held back by cancer. My "I Will Conquer" attitude, my faith, and supportive family and friends got me through the whole process.

It was only six weeks after surgery that we started six weeks of daily radiation to my head and neck. My fear of the cancer paled in comparison to the fears I had of having my head strapped down to a metal table with a plastic mesh mask tightly molded to my face, while they shot radiation through me, knowing that with each treatment, my side effects would worsen daily. After only two weeks of radiation, the blisters on my tongue, mouth, and throat, and difficulty swallowing even my own saliva resulted in a feeding tube being placed in my stomach.

The side effects were painful, but my spirits were high because I knew it was a trial I had to endure. Sometimes I just had to focus on getting through that day.

There were lessons for me to learn that I wouldn't be able to learn any other way. I decided to look for those lessons and have gratitude for the many, many blessings in my life. Every day when I had my head strapped down to the table, and I started to feel claustrophobic, I would think of all the things I was grateful for, such as family, friends, radiation staff, technology to treat this cancer, heat in the building, a sterile environment, a tile floor (instead of a dirt floor in another country), electricity for lighting, and so on.

Here is something I know about the Law of Attraction: we get what we focus on most of the time. Whatever we think about, we draw to us. This Law of Attraction is as true as the Law of Gravity. Knowing this, I was able to keep my thoughts on what I wanted, not what I didn't want. The Bible tells us, "As a man thinketh, so also he is." So we are what we think we are.

Sympathy from others was something I didn't want. I desired their encouragement and thoughts of healing instead. Because if they said, "I'm sorry you are going through all this, and you must feel miserable," I would have focused on the pain and the illness. I wanted people to give me words of healing because that's where I wanted my focus to be.

The only thing I wanted to draw to me was good health. Every day I focused on the good and exceptional health that I wanted, not the illness that I didn't want. Sometimes it was tough to do this when I was feeling crummy, but I did it anyway. I am now one year out from surgery and treatments, and so far, the doctors tell me there is no evidence of cancer and it's very unlikely it will return. I attribute much of that to a strong mindset.

One lesson I learned is to be more present in each situation I'm in, and to not be distracted. When I'm with family, I focus on my family, make eye contact with them when speaking to them, not texting my business partners or friends or worrying about all the other things I could be doing. And when I'm working my home business, helping others to achieve their goals, I focus on that and try not to get distracted. A divided mind does not serve anyone.

Another lesson I learned is that life is too short for us to be limited by our fears and to be afraid to take some risks. Too many people reach the end of their lives with regrets for the things they did not do. My passion is to live life to the fullest, to take chances, overcome my fears, and live up to the potential that God gave me so that when I get to the end of my life, I can look back and say, "Yeah, that was a life well-lived." Another passion of mine is to work with others, to help them achieve the same results.

All in all, I am grateful for my cancer journey. It was completely miserable at times, but I always knew I'd learn something from it. That God would redirect my path somehow and draw me closer to Him and my family. It cultivated me to be the wife, mom, and business leader that God created me to be. I wouldn't have experienced this level of growth without this experience.

Whatever your trial is, whether it's a health, relationship, or work situation, I challenge you to take a step back and ask yourself a few questions:

- Instead of "Why me?" ask yourself, "Why not me?"
- "What lessons am I supposed to learn as a result of going through this trial?"
- "How am I being refined?"
- "How might I be able to serve others as a result of this experience?"

Sometimes God can only get our attention by strapping us down with an illness or life obstacle. Oftentimes, it takes a painful experience that causes us to step back and evaluate what we are doing, and where we are going.

Your focus should not be on the obstacles holding you back. Instead, allow the obstacle to teach you and refine you into the person, the leader, the mom or the dad, the friend, the brother, the sister, the daughter or son that you were called to be. Each one of us was given different gifts and talents, and it is up to us to figure out what they are and to use them to the best of our abilities. Find out what it is you are called to do.

As you go through your trials, be very aware of your mindset. Refuse to let an illness or an obstacle become your identity. The Law of Attraction, says that like attracts like. If you put out negative thoughts, like "Why am I always sick?" then you will continue to have illness. Instead, focus on the end result you desire (strong health, strong marriage, success in business, living your dream life), so you can draw that to you.

Realize that you have way too many things to do on this earth than to be burdened with this trial. Know that you will be a stronger person on the other side of it. Going through these experiences will position you to mentor and help people who go through a similar experience.

Move forward in the direction of your dreams. Obstacles will certainly meet you in your path. But YOU get to decide what you do with them. Let the obstacles refine you into the person you are called to be. Don't let them cause you to give up. Don't give up... step UP!!

Compiled by Anita Sechesky

Sarah Bailey is an International Author, entrepreneur, and business consultant. She first worked as a registered dietician in major teaching hospitals, nursing homes, and in corporate nutrition. After staying home full-time with her kids for nine years, she became passionate about growing a home business, teaching others how to create the incomes and life they desire, right from the comfort of their own homes. She believes in living life to the fullest now (not waiting until retirement) and showing others how they can do the same. She lives in Connecticut with her loving husband and two very fun and growing boys.

Website: **SarahDBailey.com**

Facebook: **facebook.com/SarahDickinsonBailey**

Twitter: **twitter.com/SarahBaileyB**

CHAPTER ELEVEN

MORE Healing for the Mind
by Anita Sechesky

Our mind is the control center for the entire body, and it initiates the actions and reactions of life around us. Many people have yet to come to the knowledge and awareness of how powerful our minds really can be. Every thought we create has the profound ability to affect our lives, as these ideas become a blueprint for our minds to focus on and move forward in that direction.

Our physical responses react to our thoughts. We can literally make ourselves happy or sad and follow through with those behaviors. Since we do not know the future, why do we often think about the worst possible outcome? It is more beneficial to focus on and create positive thoughts that encourage our bodies not to have any stress or tension.

Throughout my nursing career, I have witnessed so many perplexed individuals worrying about future events they had absolutely no control over. Anxiety only causes tension, increased heart-rate, frustration and plain old stress! Many physicians would agree that it can even lead to complicated health issues if left unattended. Every area of our lives can be affected by poor eating habits, bad decision making, relationship issues, insomnia, and even affect productivity in the workplace. Who wants that?

We all have the ability to change the direction of our lives. We really can create our reality by the negative and positive thoughts that we think about. I know you can imagine all the ways that your life could be better right now. So go ahead and keep thinking better thoughts! Keep dreaming and keep focusing! Let go of all the false beliefs you thought were wasting your time in the past and start planning for the life you really want by using your mind to discover the best ways to make it happen. Are you where you want to be in life right now? If you are, then good for you! If you aren't and believe you may be stuck in a rut, you can still change your destiny. Yes! You can change it and you can continue to adjust the way that you want to respond to life.

What you focus on really does becomes your reality. What are you thinking about at this very moment? If your thoughts are about worry, stress, and hopelessness, then you will always have something more to be anxious about. But if your thoughts are on solution-based living, then you have a positive outlook and you will always find the answer that will work for you. Where there is a will, there is always a way. Many times, in life we don't even realize we can easily become our very worst enemy. The reason I say this is because if we continue to allow others to harm, betray or disrespect our dignity, we are letting ourselves down; no one else! So why would you want to do the very same thing to yourself that you wouldn't want others to do to you? You see, we subconsciously choose the lives we have. We all have choices to make and we determine the outcome of our decisions by what we want or choose to avoid in this life. When we have a sound mind, we consciously and sub-consciously choose to make informed and solid decisions healthy based on our internal dialogue, which are the words we keep feeding our spirits. As we choose the words we speak and focus on, it helps us to make right or wrong decisions that will bring healing or stress to our lives and ultimately affect our productivity and personality. This is what also assists us to fit into our present circumstances with confidence and more positive results that allows us the responsibility in how we live our lives. Sometimes it may be as simple as just needing to fall in love with ourselves all over again. Many may not even understand what I am saying, but it is a very healthy thing to discover that you love yourself and the life that you have based on how you address everything that comes your way.

Once you begin to accept the circumstances in your world, you will continually see the details for anything with a renewed perspective. It may be that the life you once thought was so horrible is not so bad after all. For some, it might be a wake-up call to discover their best life to live yet! Either way, loving oneself can sometimes be compared to Godliness as God created you in HIS image. Be thankful you were created as the beautiful, handsome, gorgeous and wonderful human being that you are. After all, you could have ended up being on the other end of the food chain!

Over the years I have met so many amazing people in my profession as an RN, Professional Coach and Publisher and I must admit that I've also seen how people, in general, have so much on their minds, with no resolution in sight. They are often filled with so many responsibilities, sometimes more than they should have taken on as a result easily lose sight of reality don't know how to enjoy life anymore. They end up coming into the hospital with some ailment or infirmity, because of poor life management skills and a very weak support system. Their daily tasks have finally become so overwhelming and they just lose that spark and zest for living. You see, they have allowed the burdens and all its negative energy just to pile up and become impossible to find any light at the end of their tunnel. They may even have developed a stress-related illness: another thing to worry about on top of everything else.

We all have roles and responsibilities, but is it fair to make yourself forget how fun and carefree life can be? Many times it can be as simple as taking the time to relax once in a while. Yes, there will always be things to do, but I often wonder why people get so bent out of shape because they have to take the garbage out or maybe do something extra today. What about the grumpy co-worker who doesn't care about who they offend or hurt?

Our minds have the ability to block out all of these negative events and its effects in life if we want to or choose to. Energy is powerful, and it is responsive to our thoughts and the words that we speak. By choosing to keep a healthy balance in life, many people can easily start gaining back their control over so many lost opportunities to living without limitations by forgiving themselves and others. They can shift the way they look at themselves and how amazing they really are. Trust me, I have been there, and I have had to do this exact same thing. Yes, I made up my mind that I would be positive and not attract anything harmful into my world. Besides, I did not want that draining, negative energy to come near me and make my day stressful. As a nurse, I had to learn how not to sponge it up. By doing so, I remained calm and full of peace, positivity, and smiles! In healthcare, there are many opportunities to do this very thing when working with so many people who carry their emotional baggage into every room they walk into. I encourage you to stop being an emotional sponge; your mind can create more of what you want in your life. What you focus on can become your reality!

Here are some more tips to help heal your mind and keep it healthy:

- let go of all the things from your past that do not empower

you to become a better person.
- let go of relationships that are verbally damaging.
- let go of addictions that may be keeping you in a place of dependence.
- let go of negative self-talk.
- let go of the reasons why you think you don't deserve better.
- let go of the self-hate and self-abuse
- let go painful memories
- let go of what does not serve you any longer.
- let go of lost hope.
- let go of social activities that attract nonsense.
- let go of the abusive relationships
- let go of the words that others have spoken against you.
- let go of the painful memories you keep replaying in your mind.
- let go of all the lies told by others.
- let go of fears.
- let go of rejection.
- let go of places that remind you of painful events.
- let go of pictures and memories from past broken relationships.
- let go of things that remind you of failures.
- let go of the past; it is not where you are going.

Here are some things you will want to remember to keep your mind healthy:
- Receive Love!
- Give love!
- Forgive yourself.

- Forgive others.
- Show appreciation to others.
- Think Success!
- Associate with Positivity!
- Discover new and healthy relationships!
- Be kind to yourself.
- Be your Best Friend Forever!
- Forgive yourself.
- Read inspirational material.
- Attend things you enjoy.
- Pursue your passions.
- Give yourself a chance to make mistakes; you are only human.
- Learn to laugh at yourself and then laugh every day.
- Live light-hearted.
- Listen to uplifting music.
- Read the comics.
- Observe the elderly.
- Watch your children and learn from them how to enjoy life through the eyes of a child.
- Spend more time with your family.
- Spend more time with your parents.
- Assess your relationships and discover the draining ones.
- Make the right decisions that you have been putting off for so long.
- Be confident!
- Understand yourself.

- Research your doubts.
- Share your life with those you care about.

I urge you to take control of your mind. Don't just let life happen to you. Steer it in the direction that you want it to go. Refocus and zoom in on your long-lost goals. Examine the lives of others that you admire and observe their behaviors and choices closely. Let life show you how you can succeed and make things happen effortlessly without the stress and turmoil of ignorance.

You are a highly intelligent creature with a powerful mind. You are capable of moving forward successfully. Failures can become a stepping stone to learn from your past mistakes. Be mindful. Allow yourself the room to grow into your best self yet!

Anita Sechesky

Anita is the Brampton Chapter President of the Holistic Chamber of Commerce because she believes in supporting all entrepreneurs who work from a mind, body & spirit perspective. As a Registered Nurse with over twenty years in Health Care, she has worked with all age groups and diversities.

Anita has excellent written, and communication skills is empathetic and goal-oriented. She is as an ICF - Certified Professional Coach, Publisher, Law of Attraction Practitioner, and soon-to-be Master of NLP Practitioner, as well as a #1 and multiple Best-Selling author.

Email: **lwlclienthelp@gmail.com**

Website: **www.lwlpublishinghouse.com**

Compiled by Anita Sechesky

CHAPTER TWELVE

I Am a Soul Survivor: Healing from Depression and Self-Abuse

by Kaila Janes

Depression is often a life filled with silence. Some may think that depression is deliberately chosen. It is just a way you think or feel. That it can be changed just by thinking or feeling different. This is not the truth. I have lived with depression for eleven years. I know what it is like to be taken over by the feelings it brings upon the person who suffers from it. I have lived through the days where all I wanted to do was lie in bed and shut the world out. I know what it's like to hit rock bottom.

As a Christian, I would wear masks which hide the sadness. It was all because I feared being judged. Aren't Christians supposed to be happy people? Don't they have God on their side? While this may be true, God doesn't cause depression. It is an imbalance within and can affect anyone of any age, religion or race just the same. It doesn't pick and choose one person over another.

Most of my life I just wanted to crawl into a hole, curl up and disappear. Spending my life faking happiness and smiling when deep down all I felt was despair was the most difficult show to put on. One of my loved ones once said to me, "You have failed in life!" This statement stabbed me in the heart to the deepest core, making me only shut down further. The emotional pain of those words was so intense, I didn't truly know how to deal with them or cope with the effects they created within.

The depression began to take over my entire life and I began finding release in cutting. At first, it started slowly. Then there were days I would get so depressed that all I could think about was cutting my wrist. There was one night in particular that stands out in my mind. Family drama swirled around, engulfing me in negativity.

I felt so defeated, all alone; like no one cared I was even there. I sat on my bedroom floor, darkness surrounding me, knife in my hands. I just cried out to God to take my life! I didn't want to be a part of this world any longer.

It was a nonstop battle in my mind. The smallest things would seem to trigger it. Whether it was my parents fighting, someone yelling at me, loved ones moving away, or even having a broken family, it created the perfect storm within. Being an emotional sensitive type of person, I didn't have the tools to adequately deal with these situations in a healthy manner. I would tend to bottle everything up inside instead of reaching out for help from others. Even when I did, it seemed to get me nowhere. Unfortunately, the only way I found relief was cutting.

At the age of twenty-four, I started my first medication. After three days I stopped. I didn't like the side effects, how the medication made me feel. It drained me of every ounce of energy, which only kept me in the depressed state. There were days I felt like a hypocrite. Here I was supposed to be living a Godly life and yet many nights I found myself trying to think of ways to end the precious life He had given to me. Scars were created by my actions. These scars were the most difficult evidence of my depression to hide. Even though I never made really deep cuts, they were still quite noticeable.

Men were a source of great pain for me, starting with my father. The pain carried through into my relationships and friendships with other men as I grew up. I found myself giving my heart away to people who claimed they were friends but really in the end only wanted one thing. It caused my heart deep pain to know that someone I loved so deeply didn't love me back. It made me feel unwanted, unacceptable and lonely. I tried to fill the void within me with relationships, but the heartache was only another source that dragged me further into my depressive state.

My life was going in a downward spiral, and I felt all I could do was watch it happen. My faith started to crumble, I felt so far from God. I didn't know who I was anymore. My life was a battlefield! I didn't know which battles to continue to fight and which ones to just give into.

Depression isn't the end of my story. It doesn't define who I am and it doesn't define who you are either. It is a condition, but it is not who you are! Living with depression and self-injury has made me a stronger person. It gave me the drive to help others. I look at my life just a year ago and I can't even imagine that I would be in the place I am now. The transformational journey is where I live currently. It is a path. The temptation to cut is there, just like any addiction or condition, but I have learned coping mechanisms. I have a support system I am always building around me. They lift me up and listen intently to what I have to say no matter what. I am not judged, just accepted, which gives me the endurance to push through to fight back. There are so many people in my life who love me and see something special when they look at me. I learned to stop being so hard on myself. I learned that I have a great personality, am worthy of so much more than I know, and am a person full of laughter. I deserve happiness; I deserve to shine, just as you who read this do! Sometimes we may be our own worst enemies.

I have been given the opportunity to reach out to others by sharing my story. Survival would not have happened if I hadn't noticed the need for love. Not the love of a man but the love of my heavenly father. Words carry more power than you know. Words can help save a life; they can build people up or tear them down. It took me a long time to realize just how important it was to forgive myself and to ask for the Lord's forgiveness. I needed to love myself in order to truly love those around me. Change doesn't happen overnight. It takes small steps. Even if you have to wake up every morning, look in the mirror and say, "I am worth it," or "Thank you Lord for life today," it makes a difference. Every small action leads to larger actions.

Many roadblocks have been placed before me along my healing journey. I know there is light at the end of the tunnel; I can see it shinning in my life. There is hope! Believe it! No matter how difficult it may seem right now, this is only but a moment, and change takes just that one step in the direction you want to go. Surround yourself with people who encourage you and lift you up. Positivity breeds positivity and negativity breeds negativity. Think of your dreams and the things you want in life. Make those dreams a reality! It is possible!

I will not let depression or cutting control my life. I am worth the fight. The scars I bear only remind me that the Lord is the reason I am alive today. I am a survivor and that will never change.

5 steps you can take immediately to begin a life of change!

1. Isolation is desolation! Do not stay isolated! Surround yourself with positive people, people who listen and love you no matter

what.

2. Professionals are there to help you. Seek out a counselor, psychologist or life coach for your specific needs. A family doctor can help point you in the right direction if you don't know where to start.

3. Find healthy ways in which to express yourself. Ways that can bring you happiness within and fill that void. Examples can be music, writing, movies, etc.

4. If you feel the need to cut or do other self-destructive behaviors, reach out to your support network. Don't be alone or isolate yourself.

5. Get involved in your community through youth groups, or other church groups. Being involved in your community can create a sense of accomplishment.

Remember to live, love and laugh! You are not alone in this fight. There are others who struggle just like you. It is time to break those chains that bind you and live a life of freedom! The life God truly created for you. There is a plan for you, your life is worth living and change is one step towards a different destination. Be the change, be the voice, don't let your life be defined by where you have been.

Kaila Janes is a certified Law of Attraction Practitioner, International Author, Inspirational Speaker, and Motivational Trainer. For the past four years, she has worked as a Medical Office Assistant where she's had to overcome quite a few challenges. She is also writing a novel about her life and the hurdles that she needed to overcome. Kaila enjoys writing and finding ways to make a difference in people's lives. Her other interests include singing and anything music related. Kaila loves to laugh and truly believes laughter is the best medicine.

Twitter: **twitter.com/godsmonkey22**

Facebook: **Kaila E. Janes**

Email: **kaila.janes@yahoo.ca**

More Stories to Heal Your World Now

Compiled by Anita Sechesky

CHAPTER THIRTEEN

Yes, I Can Be Sweet as Chocolate
by Anita Sechesky

When I was growing up in Terrace Bay, a small community in North-western Ontario, I recall wondering "Why did we come here?" I will never forget the early years of feeling like I didn't belong or fit in growing up in such an isolated part of Canada.

I was born in Georgetown, the exotic and tropical country of British Guyana. My family relocated to the extreme cold winter climate of Canada when I was only 4 years old. This was my first major life transition. I can still remember being in the change room in public school with all the girls looming over me because I had pierced ears. I guess at that time it wasn't a Canadian "thing" for little girls to have their ears pierced at such a young age. They kept asking me what kind of language I was speaking since my Guyanese accent was very different to them. Even though they understood me, they questioned everything I was saying. Some of my classmates would even stand next to me and compare their pale skin to my golden-brown skin tone. "Yes, I was the new kid in town and I was Brown." I recall being placed one year ahead of my Canadian peers in class because when I lived in Georgetown, I had already attended nursery school so I knew my "ABC's", "123's" and cursive writing. I was left-hand by birth, but had to change and learn to write with my right hand because this is what was now expected.

The novelty of being the new kid eventually wore off. No child should ever feel isolated or alone. I recall many times walking home by myself and talking to Jesus. HE was my best friend and never let me down. I remember during recesses being the only one out on the school grounds by myself. All the other kids kept to themselves, playing at the other end of the school yard. I was never invited to join them. That was when the "Lonely Years" began for me in Grades 4 and 5. Ironically, it was a period in my life that I made a significant discovery of my life's purpose. From this age, I decided that when I grew up, I wanted to be a Registered Nurse just like my late aunt. Despite being teased by a few of my classmates because of the color of my skin, or being called "Brownie" or "Chocolate", I felt sorry for these people who didn't understand that despite our exterior differences, all people from all over the world had the same emotions and feelings and therefore deserved to be treated equally. What a profound discovery at such a young age. I strongly believe that I owe my philosophical views on life to my mom and dad, who themselves were dealing with adult ignorance in a small "white" community. Many people in this part of the country had no shame in their outward prejudices or indifference to something that was not like them. My parents taught me to forgive others despite the circumstances we faced.

When I was nine years old, my cousins from Toronto moved in with us. I remember asking my older cousin, as she was making these amazing chocolate cookies with REAL chocolate bars, "Why do they call me Chocolate?" She smiled at me, said "Because you are so sweet Anita!" and gave me a hug. That is a moment I will never forget. Yes, I am sweet and yes, I can be smart.

If you ask me what the worst was, I would have to say that my bad days were the lonely times I spent by myself. When the other kids were invited to birthday parties, my invitation never seemed to arrive. One specific time, I remember my neighbour across the street from where I grew up looked like he invited the entire class at his house, but I wasn't. It was a horrible feeling witnessing this because I felt like I didn't fit in once again even though we were good friends when we were much younger. The only reason I mention this is because the previous years when his family first moved to town, we were great friends doing cart wheels on the front yard or just hanging out on our bikes with the other kids in the neighbourhood. His family moved away and later that year, he came back for a visit. It was the last time I saw him because a few weeks after he went home he died. This event left me realizing how fragile life really is and that even though friendships may not last forever, the impact that we have on one another's lives last for eternity. My late childhood friend had shown me that how easily our perceptions are influenced by others and despite everything; I could still be accepted for who I was regardless of where I came from.

When I got into the older grades, I am thankful for some very close and dear friends who helped me develop my unique personality. We had some great times together going through High School. As crazy as those days may have been as a teenager, joking and laughing, life felt more care free because I was learning how having a certain attitude of positivity can go a long way.

As the years went by, I realized that not all people were as nice and sweet as I thought. It is a sad testament to what many were exposed to and the ignorance they chose to stay in. My faith in God helped me through so many times when I did not understand even those who betrayed my loyalty in the Church. Many people may attend a church, but they may not always have the love of God within their hearts. Because of faith, I learned from an early age to forgive others not because I was supposed to but because it really did make me feel better inside. It didn't matter if they were family, friends, people I knew, or complete strangers, I learned that no one has the right to make me feel badly for who I was because greater is He that is within my heart than what happens around me. This set the course and direction for my life. Without actively practicing the Love of God and applying forgiveness when needed, I could never have made it through some of the most hurtful experiences in my life.

For those of you who have experienced similar feelings of isolation, rejection, or racism, I want to encourage you. If you see a need for racial tolerance, approach your employer or community organizations and help new citizens integrate successfully. After all, each person brings a promise of hope and richness to society.

Just because you may not necessarily fit into the environment you are in right now, it doesn't mean that you can't flourish or become all that you were created to be. You are an incredible creation. There's only one of you: individual, unique, and wonderfully made. You have your own fingerprints, feelings, emotions, and memories. I urge you to let go of what harm others have said or acted out towards you. Ignorance is a weapon that many do not understand that causes division and turmoil.

Do not let the hatred of others take your joy away. Let go of things that do not allow you the freedom to love yourself. Seek out counsel when necessary and believe that not all people are the same. Many negative behaviours and attitudes are developed because of geographical locations and upbringing. Unfortunately, because not all individuals are educated enough to understand humanity, appreciation for different cultures lack within these people.

It's time to explore your heart. What is it that you desire in life? You've been given a chance to live the best life as you see fit. We all start from somewhere, but end up in a different place. Don't be so hard on yourself; you have greatness waiting to be discovered within. Listen to your heart, mind, body, and spirit. Let them be your compass for your greatest discovery. Re-examine your life. Where are you? Is it where you want to be? If it is, then why are you still unhappy? You can always start new tomorrow. Develop a game plan for your life. Set yourself up for success. Think baby steps, then you can leap tall buildings. Your healing begins now. Your past does not determine your future, in fact your past discovers your future if you use the pieces of your life as the stepping stones to your personal success. No matter what culture you are, you are the culture of God, our Creator as you were created in HIS image. Love yourself. What better way to be your own BFF (Best Friend Forever). Now is the time to start dreaming, start believing, start praying, and start expecting great things to happen. It's about time; you deserve it.

I would love to work with you. As a Certified Professional Coach, I can help you to move quickly into the life of your dreams than if you were to walk this road alone.

Anita is the Brampton Chapter President of the Holistic Chamber of Commerce because she believes in supporting all entrepreneurs who work from a mind, body & spirit perspective. As a Registered Nurse with over twenty years in Health Care, she has worked with all age groups and diversities.

Anita has excellent written, and communication skills is empathetic and goal-oriented. She is as an ICF - Certified Professional Coach, Publisher, Law of Attraction Practitioner, and soon-to-be Master of NLP Practitioner, as well as a #1 and multiple Best-Selling author.

Email: **lwlclienthelp@gmail.com**

Website: **www.lwlpublishinghouse.com**

Compiled by Anita Sechesky

CHAPTER FOURTEEN

I Was Only Sixteen but I Survived!
by Brian Baulch

In March 1988, the Autumn season for Australia, I was a spirited but shy sixteen-year-old boy who was eager to pursue all of what the school curriculum offered the students, however, I was still undecided which career path to go for. I appreciated what they taught us in school such as outdoor recreational education, home economics, basic computer skills, electrical and electronics classes. The real dilemma was I had no driven passion for something desirable, which offered the old school system that geared me towards a career path.

I found my co-op job experience that I completed in the local hospital as a Hygienic Health Assistant (Cleaner) more enjoyable. I thought this was more fun than schooling. My career adviser requested an appointment after getting the report back from my job at how well the employer thought I performed. Unfortunately, the career adviser said they had no vacant job available in the cooking area at the hospital, which I wanted to try, as I did love to cook at home for the family.

Unexpectedly exciting news came from my career adviser that a local large bakery in my home city required an apprentice baker. For a minute, I did not know what to say. I had quick flash clashing through my mind to choose job or school. Finally, I agreed to an interview at the bakery, and they informed me about my job expectations. What stood out was they required someone to work the night shift. At the age of sixteen, this was not the job I wanted to pursue.

A few days passed, I had not heard from the employer about the apprenticeship or the result of my interview. I knew there were a few others going for this opportunity. Abruptly out of nowhere, I got a phone call asking if I would be ready to start on a certain date and time. Utterly gobsmacked for about fifteen seconds, I agreed to willingly venture this apprenticeship probationary period of three months.

Unknowing at the time, I clinched the deal to my first future employer that would eventually lead to a fork in the road that would change my life, despite my uncertainty about career choice. This choice would reroute my life emotionally, mentally and spiritually.

It was prevalent in the late 1980s in the Australian school system for students to leave before they completed high school to get a job or apprenticeship in the trade industry; I was one of those young people who left school at 16 years of age to discover my future goals. However, my first day at work overwhelmed me. It was literally sweltering physical work around the bakers' ovens baking bread – not to mention the five p.m. to one a.m. nightshift. It was physically daunting for me as a young person still finding his way in the world. In a matter of days, I soon discovered there was no point trying to build relationships with my co-workers. Most of the workers got angry with me when I did something incorrectly as a first timer. Some of the workers thrived on bullying me with power and words because of their higher position in the company. They seemed proud and bullied me no matter how I felt or how it affected my performance!

I recall trying to toughen up as a young man, brushing off their sarcastic remarks. I often smiled or laughed back at their faces as they continued the bullying and harassment. I remember workers often chatting and joking, which I accepted as a joke about what they termed "mate ship initiation." They often curtailed when I spoke back, "Why do such silly thing?" Then professed that every apprentice has gone through this initiation process. I was amazed when they brought this subject up!

At work embarked as a good night went well. While working at the bakery the darkest night of my job life set out to transform me in how I would see life and people around me over time. Once we finished production, we would usually start cleaning until next shift would take over from us. Without warning, four to six men workers against one altogether grabbed me – how cowardly! On average most of the workers were at least ten to fifteen years older than me.

I will never forget the feeling of the deranged darkness swallowed me up swiftly. At the time, I felt like how water drains its way down the plughole! I screamed, yelled and swore at those assaulting older men to let me go but they continued to force me to the ground. It felt like my whole world or any thought of its existence had all frozen in time and I had no control over what was taking place!

It happened so quickly I was trying to break free from the forceful grip on me. In that moment, they threatened me to make things worse if I would not let them do what they planned, in order to be part of their own working organization!

Even tho the men were stronger than me I did not give up when they pinned me to the ground. They pulled down my pants, I tried to kick them off yet but they kept pouring a thick syrupy mixture of bread making ingredients all over my private parts and legs helplessly with force.

After my harassment from those men was finally ended they let me go because they got what they wanted, even tho they freed me. I tried not to cry. I ran but found it hard to put my pants on because of the sticky syrups! I shamefully made my way back to the locker room. Some of the female staff and management observed me but they acted like it was a joke.

At the end of my three months probationary period, "I was told I was unsuitable for nightshifts." In contrast, I have been a shift-worker for over twenty-three years. I've learned to FORGIVE them all.

Sixteen Inspirational Compass Guide:

1. Speak up and try to share your bullied experience with others that you trust especially if you don't have family support or they have lack of understanding which may be due to lack of education, generational gap or social awareness on their part. Otherwise, report it to authorities.

2. Master the art of forgiving those who have harmed you verbally, spiritually, physically or holistically. Your abundance growth is vital despite the uninvited scenarios to keep you growing robustly.

3. Fear not and explore your boundaries. Unearth hidden gems to unveil new perspectives connecting the dots. My life experiences besides what I partly shared with you inspired me courageously when I realized there are many victims of

bullying, physical abuse, emotional wounds and cyberbullying these days.

4. Believe in what you can do towards your dreams no matter what episodes ahead of you and use them as your wings to mount from within yourself.

5. Be the VICTOR from those coward bullies! Connect and surround yourself with friendly like-minded people, mentors, coaches, and counselors who will always empower you towards enlarging your passion, dream, and vision.

6. Reframe your life situations and life events to align your values with healthy relationships. Imagine your ability to identify the unlabelled opportunity rather than overlooking any barren narrow road.

7. Flourish in those moments of relationships with your family and friend circles, whom you have learned to trust and who inspired you. Apply the practice of timeout from all the stressful distractions from your dreams and goals for at least one day per week or so.

8. You are born to WIN life's battle each day by the great Creator's amazing grace! When there is growth reaching towards your goals, you are in your compass zone trailblazing on your journey.

9. Learn to sustain your solitary journey at the present listening to our Divine given intuition. Discern the traveler's path of your inner intuition compass circumnavigating in the daily events of life.

10. Cultivate the art of listening and seeking wisdom, insightful books, articles and the Creator's nature around us.

11. Own the keys to your kingship mindset. Believe they are like king and queen. Learn to rule them by taking ownership you choose from each key rather than letting others choose for you.

12. Be confident. Engage and comprehend nonverbal communication with people in your social connections.

13. You are MIRACLE from your mother's womb! Your unique crafted life story exists to unleash within you.

Compiled by Anita Sechesky

14. You are INSPIRATIONAL, dare to pursue!

15. You are the MASTERPIECE! You are GREATER than your challenges when you look back at them!

16. You are the key to your successful journey; it is not all about the destination but the experiences in life-travel that count.

I hope that as you travel along the rough paths, you will define the greatest strengths within you to survive the unforeseen life-travel experiences ahead.

Brian Baulch lives in Ballarat City, Victoria, Australia and has been married for more than twelve years, although childless by no choice. He is a certified Life Coach, Newspaper Media Printers Assistant, and Owner/Co-founder with his wife of Rechargelife and Fusiontourism. His expertise led him to coach and consult small travel tourism business owners and keen travelers in connecting their mission of life experiences, expertise, passions, talents, and skills by using the information technology tools to share their unique life stories. Brian thrives on reaching out to dreamers and clients seeking a meaningful and creative-purpose life.

Website: **www.brianbaulch.com**

Email: **brianbaulch@brianbaulch.com**

Skype: **brindel**

Facebook: **Facebook.com/brianbaulchs**

Instigram: **Instagram.com/brianbaulch**

Twitter: **Twitter.com/brianbaulch**

Pinterest: **Pinterest.com/brianbaulch**

LinkedIn: **au.Linkedin.com/in/brianbaulch**

More Stories to Heal Your World Now

CHAPTER FIFTEEN

In Search of Healing
by Afya Ashiki

I am a first generation Canadian born in Toronto, Ontario, Canada. My parents immigrated from Jamaica and met here in Toronto. I love both my parents, and I know they did their best with the tools they were given. I blame no one as there is so much beauty and abuse equally on all levels that is intertwined within the culture. I was blessed to be raised by both parents as they were legally married. Standing from the outside looking in, it all appeared so perfect. They worked steady jobs, we traveled, dressed well, and joined extracurricular activities. Despite all these comforts I, unfortunately, had very low self-esteem. I know my parents will be offended, but I must tell my story. I'm recounting my experience the way I perceived my life with the hope I can help another soul out there. My goal is to empower someone to be a victor and not a victim.

Are you living with guilt and shame from concealing secrets? I did this for about fifteen years. I held a secret out of fear of being judged. I struggled with the doubts of it being my fault. I was ashamed and filled with blame for many years. These were the thought forms from hell that only led me down a path of self-destruction and self-hatred. I was volatile and easily angered. I was verbally and physically abusive, especially to my boyfriends. I did drugs and alcohol. I was addicted to sex and porn. No one looking in was aware because I was a functional addict. I lost apartment after apartment, yet I was fortunate not to become homeless or live in shelters. I refused to allow anyone to come too close to me because I saw everyone as a threat and I was fearful of showing my true colors. I lied about who I really was. I continuously hide behind my ability to articulate and dress up to the trends. Inside I felt like the ugly duckling. The overflow of compliments meant nothing.

In an instant, I lost all virtue, innocence, dignity, and self-respect was stolen. It continued, and of course, my numbing and detachment continued. I was convinced that it was okay. I was never able to have an honest conversation during girl talk about my first time. The authentic Denise died and became a farce. I had no idea who I was.

The catalyst to my healing began in my mid-twenties. I lost my second apartment and managed to rent a basement apartment from some friends. I met this beautifully spirited man from Africa who became a great go-to person as a source of fun and escaping my reality. It appeared as though he treated me with respect and replaced my name Denise with Queen, which was foreign to me but I embraced it eventually. We partied, and he was not afraid to introduce me to his friends. He cooked for me and bought me gifts. I respected him at that time. I felt as though a new experience emerged and it felt really good in the beginning. I allowed him to have sex with me without any commitment; however, he was the catalyst for my healing. One day after sex he said, "Queen, may I ask you something?" I replied "Yes," with ease not expecting to be triggered. "What happened to you when you were a child? I want to know because you are so beautiful from the inside out but I see confusion, fear, I see shame, and I see you hiding something" I was surprised...and I was speechless. Before I responded, he told me his story about being sexually abused. His story broke down my walls. My heart became lighter in knowing I was not the only one. My respect for him surpassed what it was because he created a platform for my release. He handed me the keys to free myself from my self-imposed prison. I told him the truth. It felt so good to relate to someone else. I still had a long way to go. I had a bad habit of pushing people away who encouraged me to be better when I wasn't ready. I pushed this gentleman away and sank right back into my comfort zone. I was not prepared to let go of my drug of choice. Along my journey I lost more homes, I lost my first two daughters, and I went to anger management sessions because it would help my case, not because I believed I was angry. I got up and fell again and again. Then in 2017, I turned forty years old, and my eldest daughter and I celebrated together. Three weeks later she told me she was pregnant.

My love for them and my constant breast pains were not enough for me to save myself. In solitude one day I had a divine intervention. I thought, "Wow, I am going to be a grandmother!" I had to change.

This little soul's spirit was the greatest encouragement for me to stop all destructive thinking, talking, and living. On July 5th, 2017, I stopped smoking drugs and went into rehab on July 13th for an eighteen-day program. I was privileged to meet others who wanted to live and whose childhoods were very similar. Our common denominator was not only the drugs but the trauma, guilt, and shame we were addicted to escaping from. To date, I am eight months clean and am looking forward to my first birthday – July 5, 2018. As mentioned earlier, I was a functional addict who was able to work, go to school, be an entrepreneur, facilitate my own office space, mentor youth and assist women in labor. In fact, I lacked the discipline, courage, and integrity to practice what I preached. Many times I did not show up, not only in my life but in my clients' lives as well. Many believed in me, yet they had no idea I did not believe in myself. I am still a work in progress. I am convinced my true recovery will continue as I serve others. When I finally changed the channel and played a different movie, my paradigm shifted dramatically. I am attracting beautiful, encouraging individuals and experiences that are conducive to this new life I am creating for myself. I no longer attract pimps, hustlers, and addicts.

This chapter is dedicated to all the women, especially black women, who refrain from showing up in Alcoholics Anonymous, Narcotics Anonymous meetings, and rehabilitation centers because of the fear of being stigmatized, and all the women and men who live in low-income neighborhoods who have lost hope. This chapter is devoted to others who lost their children to the system and feel as though they are a disappointment and do not deserve love; people who spend their lives playing the same movies in their heads because the coping skills were not given to them; people who keep failing continuously. I am telling you: DO NOT QUIT! Do not give up. The desire for better is your beautiful higher-self talking to you. You are reading this for a reason. If I can do it, you can too. I was not born into a wealthy family. My parents never bought and owned a house. We always lived in low-income housing and areas. We lived in a condo in the Jane and Finch area. Nothing was given to me. I guess my spirit guides knew I am here to serve and help women to embrace their higher selves. Get the help you need; you do not need to be a slave anymore. Your spirit guides led you to read this chapter. You are worthy and deserving of the very best.

Afya Ashiki has been a practicing birthing doula through DONA (Doulas of North America) since 2005. She currently works as a postpartum doula, feeding newborns at night for women who received C-sections. Ashiki is continuing her education to become a midwife and is the visionary of the upcoming anthology "The Doula Diaries."

Compiled by Anita Sechesky

WORDS OF ENCOURAGEMENT

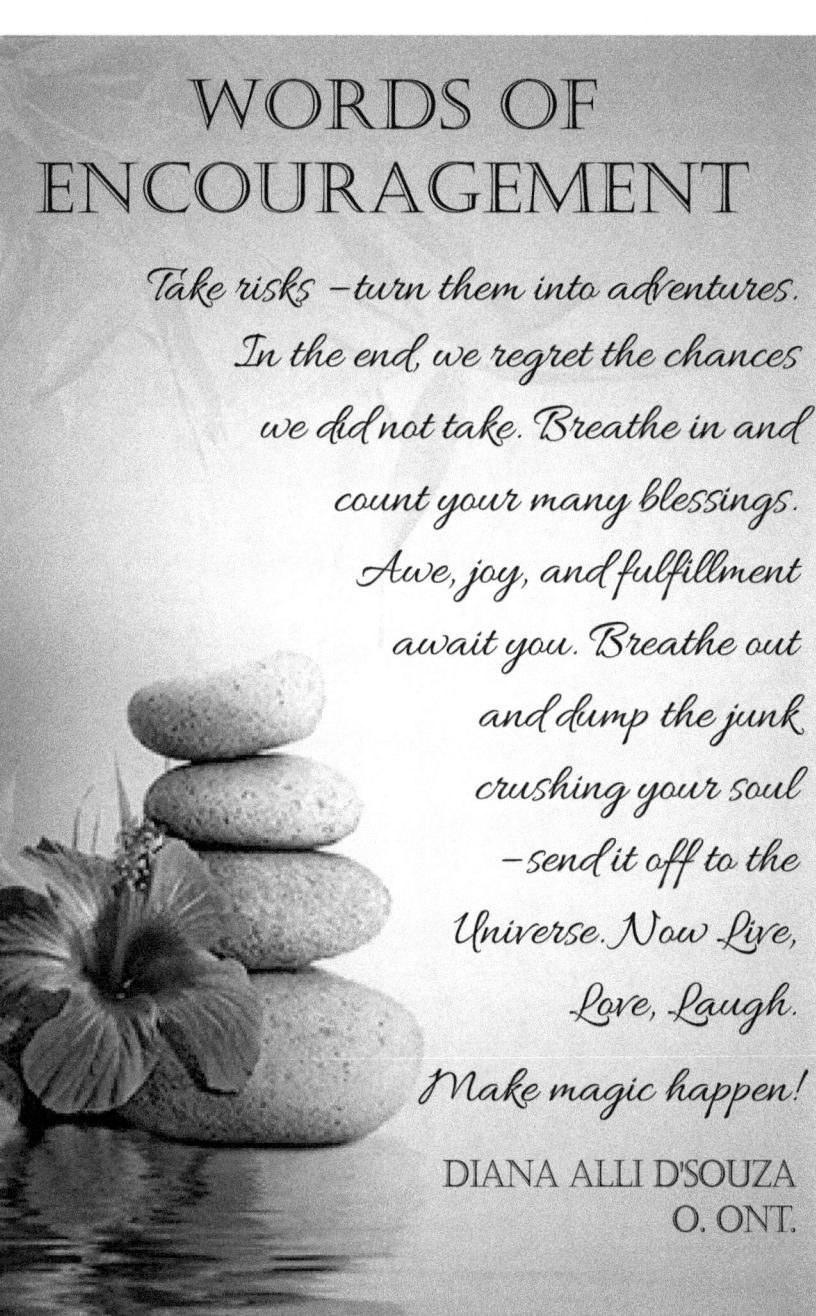

Take risks — turn them into adventures. In the end, we regret the chances we did not take. Breathe in and count your many blessings. Awe, joy, and fulfillment await you. Breathe out and dump the junk crushing your soul — send it off to the Universe. Now Live, Love, Laugh.

Make magic happen!

DIANA ALLI D'SOUZA
O. ONT.

Compiled by Anita Sechesky

CHAPTER SIXTEEN

Life's Energy Can Heal You
by Christopher Fink

One cannot talk about emotional issues and not mention mental, as they both go hand in hand, and dealing with them can involve as many similar, yet, diverse solutions. Bring in energy work, and the techniques to help doubles the chances of success in a very-much more energy-charged world.

As an energy/Reiki master with experience in psychology, along with having emotional issues of my own, it took time to figure out the connections...and found they are both biological, and psionic (mental). The exploration of both brought me to one question: What was the key connection, the starting point that I could base my own self-treatment from? The baseline point is: that emotion is energy, and knowing what I knew from my own experiences, I could bring in techniques to help myself and others, to help them through their own pain.

Let's start with the mental and emotional; then we can move on to the practical aspect of how to help yourself. As I mentioned before, both are intertwined very heavily. The biggest thing to not think is that it's all in your head – far from it, but part of it is. External factors like seeing someone hurting, hearing a crowd laughing, smelling a scent that invokes memories, or even feeling a pet's fur, can sometimes leave you bewildered, smiling, or crying all because of a response that triggers both mental and emotional aspects. Stress can prompt a mental response, that can trigger other aspects too, but it ultimately begins on the mental side.

To use energy in both aspects, let's take an example of seeing and hearing someone crying. A lot of the time if you're like me, you feel sorry for them. You want to help, and you want to ask them questions. Using energy, you can sense what's going on before you even ask anything. Ground yourself and prepare if the response is more then you expect (this highly effective with first responders of all stripes) and you can heal yourself using energy healing (IF properly trained). Do not attempt unless you are trained; trust me on this).

Another example might be that you're out on a date, doing something totally exciting, even attending a wedding and you're having a good time, or something close to it, and you want to take a moment to breathe (and be able to think). Grounding in this case, using your senses to feel the moment with introspection and seeing the world around you with a wider perspective, should be done with awareness – a technique I'll demonstrate very shortly.

I'll go into shielding too in a moment. Look at the previous two examples and see if they make sense. You're primarily using energy to hold to the moment, to calm yourself, to ready yourself for something, and to be able to help someone. These skills are helpful in a lot more situations, so on that note, let's learn the skills.

Using GSA, a technique I developed over the years, is the first thing that I teach my students. GSA means Grounding, Shielding, and Awareness, and is 100% critical to energy work. It's done in four parts (like barbershop music, and all four together are fantastic).

To start the first aspect, Grounding, make sure you're sitting, standing, or laying down – whatever you're comfortable with. See yourself as a tree and then reach down with your roots, going as deep as you can. Now, reach up with your branches, either figuratively or if you want to raise your arms, that's up to you. Now, breathe in through your branches and out through your roots. Do it gently and repeat a few times until you feel more focused and "grounded." This helps emotionally as you're more focused, calmer, and better able to see a situation through clearer eyes and thoughts. I use this multiple times a day and whenever I feel overwhelmed.

Shielding, the second aspect, is much like the shields on a sci-fi starship. Once again, get comfortable in whatever position. Now, gently stretch your arm away from you, whichever way you want to stretch it. Feel as if there is a bubble coming from the inside out, coming to a point on your fingertips, and hold it there for a moment. Do it again until you feel like it's a solid object. Now feel yourself being protected from negative emotions, a situation you may be in, or something that you see/feel/hear/touch/smell. The real benefit to shields is that your mind feels the shield, your senses are picking it up, and it allows you to dampen or ignore the emotional/mental response so you can keep going, at least until you can rest.

Awareness is the third aspect. Awareness is usually associated with only your eyes and what you see. The truth is that it's far beyond your eyes, but a combination of using your senses to their highest ability and beyond.

This is where you try to sense down to your arm and then stretch beyond, going inch by inch beyond until you feel an energy bubble around you (much like shielding). Now try to touch something close and see if you can sense it before you touch it. Do this with all types of objects. This is also the beginning of sensing energy from objects. The same skill can be used in situations where you get a "vibe." Try to stretch your senses so that you're picking up more and more. This is the hardest skill of the three to learn, but also opens up new avenues of sensing anything differently.

Integration is where you combine all of them together in the GSA order. It takes time to learn, but with practice and with trusting yourself, you will get there.

Emotions and mental health ultimately take a lot of different approaches to help manage. Through the skills that I've taught you here, hopefully I've offered a new avenue to explore which will help you through your journey. One step at a time.

Christopher Fink is currently a Technical Support Analyst with a major IT company in Hamilton, Ontario. His experience in energy work, music, and human relations have been major parts of his life. Chris has gone in many different directions, including: Barbershop Corus, Poetry, Reiki (which he's getting certified in soon), and Crisis Intervention

Compiled by Anita Sechesky

CHAPTER SEVENTEEN

My Relationship Was Red Flagged!
by Olive Walters

There seems to be a defining moment in one's life that makes such an immense impact, shakes you up and puts you on a trajectory that you might not otherwise have thought of. It is up to you to follow that path where it may lead you. ~ Olive Walters

The crash of broken glass pierced through the silence, startling me from my sleep. Heavy footsteps stomped towards my bedroom. I sat up, strained to focus on the figure who was now standing at the foot of the bed. It was then that I saw my estranged ex-boyfriend holding a knife. He dragged me out of the bedroom. He punched me repeatedly and slammed me into a glass coffee table which shattered under my weight. At one point he had me on the ground with his knee in my chest pinning me down. I had my hands wrapped around his grip on the knife and was using every bit of my strength to keep the knife from plunging into my chest. Horrible thoughts flooded through my mind of what would happen if I ran out of strength. Suddenly I heard my nine-year-old daughter scream at him "Don't kill mommy!" That startled him; he pulled away and yelled at her to go back to her room. The one thing that he kept saying over and over was "Neither one of us are leaving here alive."

I finally managed to escape and ran from the house with him close behind me. There was a police station a couple of streets away that I thought I could run to, but the combined effects of the beating, my fear, and loss of control threw me into a state of panic. In my exhaustion, I only made it a few houses away. I ran to a neighbor's and started banging on the heavy solid oak door screaming for help. Finally, after what seemed like an eternity, the owners of the house opened the door and were startled to see me bleeding, half-naked at their doorstep at 2:30 am. I knew at that moment that someone was looking over me.

Months later I could still remember thinking that nothing could have prepared me for the flood of emotions that followed that experience. Feelings ranging from shame, embarrassment, fear, hatred towards him, hatred towards myself, unworthiness, the list goes on. I felt so embarrassed and ashamed that someone who I cared for wanted me dead. I knew I didn't have the best track record in past relationships, but I kept asking myself "AM I so repulsive that emotional, psychological and physical abuse was not enough, death was what I deserved?" I felt that everyone who knew about the incident also knew that I was garbage. Intellectually I knew that his actions were not my fault, but I still tried to figure out what I did to deserve that kind of treatment. I couldn't think of anything. I just felt that I wasn't good enough, pretty enough and definitely not worthy of love. Prior to this, after each failed relationship I went through a mourning period where I scolded myself for being stupid to believe that I was worthy of love. I told myself that some people were meant to be loved and others were not. I was in the latter group. After surviving the brutal ordeal, I was even more convinced that I was not one of those lucky ones who was destined to be loved.

In the months that followed, I strived to appear like everything was normal in my world but inside I was struggling. I had nightmares every night for about year. I would see him standing at the bus stop or at the subway station waiting for me. I would have terrors of other men holding me from behind so that he could have better access to hurt me. It was as if I was trapped. I tried many ways to distract myself. I was even obsessed with watching a popular television show about inmates living in a very violent jail. I would imagine it was him getting raped, beat up, fed ground-up glass and killed. It kind of made me feel better if you can believe that. Yep, it was a dark time. It was my strange way of coping and surviving. I finally stopped watching it when a friend asked me why I was torturing myself like that. That was a major shift in my perspective. *I Woke Up* and realized it wasn't healthy. It got to the point where I couldn't stomach it anymore. I didn't want to attract those feelings much less any of those experiences.

Physically, my body was a mess. I didn't sleep more than a few hours each night and was probably underweight given that I am small framed. I felt like I was in physical pain for months, I don't know if I was just healing very slowly from the trauma or if it was more emotionally based. My menstrual cycle even stopped for six months. I was afraid all the time, whether I was on the way to or from work and definitely at home especially if my brother wasn't there. I avoided dating like the plague.

I was very fortunate though to have the people that I did in my life at the time. My boss demanded the day after the ordeal that I go into a local shelter. It was there that I got my first counseling sessions. It helped me to break off some limiting beliefs that I had embraced for so long. From there I was encouraged to seek out my support services at my place of employment and I was able to make some major shifts on my path to healing.

I had to learn to forgive myself. For what you may ask? For not listening to my inner voice. I ignored all the little signs in the beginning that told me that this relationship was not healthy. Based on my previous unhealthy relationships I didn't want to bring the wrong-doings of the last person into the new relationship...I was so worried about blaming him for things that the last guy did, that I overlooked crap that I shouldn't have. My internal protective mechanism was picking up on things but I didn't want to process them. We all have amazing inner voices. We should start listening to them. My insecurities kept me from acting on the information that I was refusing to process, from acting on what I knew I should be doing, if not for myself, then at least for my kids. I had to learn to keep forgiving myself for ignoring the signs that were actually red flags.

It wasn't an overnight process. It took years to heal from this and learn to love myself. With support from friends and loved ones especially my children, I am at a good place in my life.

Relationship Red Flags

Red Flag 1 – *Alcohol and Substance Abuse* – Please don't ignore this or make excuses for it. I made this mistake. At the court hearing he said the night he broke into my home with the knife he had drank a case of beer and it gave him the "liquid courage" he needed. **Wake up!**

Red Flag 2 – *Animosity, Anger or Racism towards Others* – If your partner has a strong hatred for groups of people, that is a major indication of turmoil in their life. How can they have the capacity to love you if they have hate for others that they do not even know? **Wake up!**

Red Flag 3 – *Blaming Others* – The man that I was involved with blamed his mother, grandmother, sister and ex-wife for all the pain in his life. He took no responsibility for any of his actions. As far as he was concerned, they were the cause of any wrongdoing on his part. **Wake up!**

Red Flag 4 – *Manipulative and Controlling* – Many abusive partners use control tactics that sound like "If you love me you will…" I heard this often. The last straw was when he said, "If you don't take me back I will kill myself." Please don't wait for it to get that far. This is not a normal healthy way to communicate with someone you love. It's a form of abuse. **Wake up!**

Red Flag 5 – *History of Damaged Relationships* – You will pick up on your partner's subtle or extreme patterns of unhealthy damaged relationships. This could be with their family or others, for example, neighbors, co-workers, classmates. Please don't ignore this. These people don't seem to have the capacity to form caring, productive and positive relationships. **Wake up!**

Dear friend, if my story resonates with you, I encourage you to use this phrase that I often use to reset my perspective. Repeat it softly to yourself when needed as often as you need.

I love you. I'm sorry. Please forgive me. Thank you.

Olive is a Law of Attraction Practitioner, Trainer, Speaker, Realtor and CEO and owner of Trecourt Virtual Services Inc. She is very passionate about the fact that she can utilize the Law of Attraction to literally create the life that she desires. She enjoys inspiring others and teaching them how to use it to create abundance and peace in their own lives. Olive is a mother, grandmother, and lover of life. With love, everything is possible.

Email: **IamOliveWalters@gmail.com**

Facebook: **facebook.com/olive.walters.90**

Twitter: **@owalters**

Pinterest: **pinterest.com/OliveWalters**

Compiled by Anita Sechesky

CHAPTER EIGHTEEN

Faith Roots Can Heal Your Future
by Koreen Bennett

Growing up in my early years with my grandparents played a huge part in establishing my personal "Faith Roots" that helped carry me through some of the worst challenges in my life.

From the age of four, I had the experience of spending four impressionable years in Jamaica with my late grandparents who left an enormous impact on my years to come. I would see my grandpa going to or coming back from the field where he would have been tending to his farm animals (cows, goats, pigs, and chickens) and coffee trees. After completing his early morning chores, he would come into the house, wash up, and eat breakfast that Grandma had cooked and had it already set on the table, knowing the exact time he would come in. After having breakfast, Grandpa would get ready to go out as he had a business and would be dressed quite dapper in his suit and fedora hat (loved seeing him in his hat). On Sundays, we (my grandparents, my sister, and I) all went to church; but even before going to there or even before having breakfast, my grandparents woke everyone in the house to have early morning devotions. Sometimes other family members who lived close by would come to our devotions. I would watch my grandpa, aunt, and uncle set up chairs and we would find our place on one or the couch to get our "mini church service" started. Everyone would sing hymns (I listened mostly as I didn't know the words to the hymns). Grandpa would read from the Bible and explain what God was saying. He then prayed. Our mini service was finished with everyone reciting a bible verse. We all sat together, ate breakfast, and then got dressed for Sunday morning church service. This was our Sunday morning routine and was mandatory in our grandparents' home. This was my first interaction with God.

My grandparents were very involved in the church. They were advisors/counselors, teachers, and prayer warriors. You could never go hungry with my grandparents around; they were a giving couple.

A seed of hope, faith, love of God and for God was planted very early. I am very thankful to my mom for sending my sister and me to my grandparents and to my grandparents for setting the foundation. There have been so many positives. I now know why I have the desires to have my own businesses, the love of helping others, and the close relationship I have with my sister. That very seed has helped me through some difficult times.

As teenagers, we did question why we had to go to church, not that we were going every Sunday anyway. It was not mandatory for us to go to church every Sunday (especially when our grandparents were not visiting). I knew there was a God but was my faith strong? I would say, no. I would kneel down at the side of my bed and say a two-minute prayer before getting into bed at nights, which I did every night, believe it or not. But did I read the Bible and go to church religiously on Sundays? No, I didn't. It was not mandatory. Again, remember, that seed was already planted. It just wasn't watered.

So life throws some curve balls and some really hard balls, but I believe if you have a real relationship with God, that relationship cushions some of those hits. One of those fast curve balls came at my family twelve years ago when we received the news that the baby I was already carrying for five months would be disabled. I didn't think I could get up from that hit, but God prepared me for what was to come. Given a medical option by my doctor, I realized there was absolutely no other alternative but to accept my gift from God.

I was told I would have to quit my nursing career and care for my baby twenty-four hours a day. I was not gaining weight normally during my pregnancy and there were abnormalities with the fluid that was supposed to be protecting him, but I was assured by my doctor that I was still pregnant. I truly had no choice but to find faith and hope in God for the first time ever in my life by realizing He was much bigger than the surreal situation and nightmare I was living. Finally, I could understand my grandparent's faith and where it was coming from. What was the alternative? The love and support of my husband and elder son were needed but all their love would not have been enough to guide me through this unexpected revelation of the health of my unborn child. Of course, I felt fear. Was my precious baby receiving all the nutrients he needed? Why was this happening? What would his life be like?

Through this season I had moments of fear, anger, and sadness of this diagnosis, but hope and love for my child. With all these emotions and uncertainty, I knew God was with me. At times I felt such calmness; it was as if I knew everything would be alright. God kept me close. I drew so much more on my faith at this moment. I did not understand then how being blessed with a special needs child would change the life of my family and the attitude towards life. How do you overcome the challenges? Believe me, no one is perfect and even I forget and lose hope and joy when I focus on the world or my circumstances. It is perfectly normal to go through many emotions during life's storms, but know that your outlook can carry you through anything. It may be hard to believe, especially if you are facing a trial right now. I was watching a television show not too long ago and the speaker said, "You are either in a storm, getting out of a storm, or going into a storm." So, where ever you are in your ordeal, hope, trust, and belief are all values you will need to go through it. Call out to God, your creator and Heavenly Father – He will hear you. Thank you so much, my friend, for stepping into my world to learn what I have healed from and now embrace with open and loving arms.

We are a part of a world that is fast-paced. We go, go, go...forgetting to STOP for a moment to even take a breath. God wants us to reach out and invite Him into our everyday lives. That's why I have created the FAITH ROOTS template below, especially for those who may be going through a diagnosis of cancer, the news that your baby will be disabled, the loss of a loved one, the loss of your home, loss of your innocence, abuse, betrayal from someone you once believed in, being rejected and the hope for a happy future. You can easily follow in whichever order you feel. We are all created in God's image, which means you are also compassionate, loving, forgiving, understanding, and empathetic. We all know the world needs more hope, faith, and love. I have learned through life experiences that the happiest and most content of people do not always have a life of perfection. They value who they are and where they come from.

FAITH ROOTS for Overcoming Life's Greatest Challenges

1. **I ENCOURAGE YOU** to take time to release through forgiveness as much of the pain, anger, frustration, disappointments, rejection, brokenness, hate, and anything that has made

you change from the person you really are inside with the peace you once knew long ago.

2. **I ENCOURAGE YOU** to motivate yourself by reading the Bible daily at least one verse a day or downloading a Bible Devotion App that will send you a simple Bible verse daily to encourage and comfort you when life's struggles are more than you may be able to bear at times on your own.

3. **I ENCOURAGE YOU** to be more observant in the things that you allow to influence your spirit because it will eventually affect your spiritual health, such as music, books you read, people you associate with, TV and movies, your social settings.

4. **I ENCOURAGE YOU** to speak positive words over your circumstances, no matter how discouraging the situation might feel because this will increase your faith and give you hope.

5. **I ENCOURAGE YOU** to speak daily Positive Affirmations (Talk to yourself. Yes! I said it. Talk to yourself!)

6. **I ENCOURAGE YOU** to do what you can to help yourself nourish your mind and heal your spirit like this book will. Please read it a couple of times if you have to because it will help you to take the focus off your situation, what you are going through, and release the stress of uncertainty.

7. **I ENCOURAGE YOU** to take care of your body by eating healthy balanced meals which includes fresh fruits and vegetables, fresh fish, seafood, whole grains, and drinking more water.

8. **I ENCOURAGE YOU** to enjoy life, take brisk nature walks, enjoy a nice warm soothing bath, having an attitude of gratitude. Take a moment to assess your environment – is it supporting your peace of mind? Are there things that have been pushed aside or not addressed such as the cleaning of the house or mending valued relationships with loved ones?

9. **I ENCOURAGE YOU** to talk openly to God regardless of where you are in your faith. There is no perfect person, but YOU ARE PERFECT IN HIS EYES and God loves you just as you are. You can even talk to Him like you would if you were talking to your best friend.

10. Like any relationship where we allow people to come into our hearts, **I ENCOURAGE YOU**, dear friend, to also take a moment to invite God's only son Jesus into your heart because Jesus loves you and he is the way to find so many things you may have lost in your life through some of your own greatest struggles such as love, joy, peace, perseverance, strength, courage, and a future filled with so much more hope than you could ever imagine right now.

I thank you so much for taking the time to go through all these FAITH ROOTS. By consistently applying these simple life applications as much as possible, God will equip you with all that you need, and you will begin to experience a renewing of who you are as well. I pray that you find the peace and comfort in knowing that through our Lord Jesus, all things are possible. **I ENCOURAGE YOU!**

Koreen Bennett is married and the mother of two sons whom she is extremely proud of. She is a Registered Nurse for fifteen years and has been working in the healthcare field for over twenty years. Koreen's varied skill set has allowed her to help people from diverse backgrounds to stay physically, emotionally, and healthy.

Compiled by Anita Sechesky

WORDS OF ENCOURAGEMENT

May your days be as bright as a ray of sun.
May each day bring you courage
to take one more step.
May the next step bring you closer
to the wisdom you seek,
the happiness you need,
the love you desire.
May each night bring
a peaceful rest blessing
for you with strength
for the new day.

ELIZABETH ANN PENNINGTON

CHAPTER NINETEEN

I Broke through the Wall of Doubt
by Patrick Hayden

Let me start this chapter by saying thanks to a woman who saw something in my words and believed I had something to share with the World. Thank you so much, Anita Sechesky; you came into my life after I had reached rock bottom. At that time I laid the new foundation for myself, giving me the spark to create light and show the World my gift. We will remain connected in the spirit of truths.

As a professional Life Coach, the discovery of breaking through the Wall of Doubt while conquering bipolar was no easy challenge but in all fairness, I had many tools. I was also working with my brother and son in our innovation company; this gave me a great foundation.

What is the Wall of Doubt? Where did it come from? How can we demolish it? Many people on the Earth experience self-sabotage by the Wall of Doubt; they feel trapped inside themselves, and thus live a poor quality of life. I can say this because I was once in those shoes.

First, let me explain to you what the Wall of Doubt is. The Wall of Doubt is constructed by you and by the influences you receive from others – meaning adults, teachers, family, and friends. Our mind has two sides, the conscious side, which is the side that wants things and the subconscious, which is the side that is connected to your spirit and abundance. As newborns our minds are pure and the two minds are connected, but as we ask questions we start to construct the Wall of Doubt between the two minds. There are two types of belief blocks that we place in the Wall of Doubt, one is brickage-beliefs, which are small beliefs and the other is blockage-beliefs, which are convictions.

These beliefs are placed in the Wall of Doubt by the questions we ask, so some of them are wrongly placed beliefs and hold us back from our true self. This self-sabotage restricts our true growth, as we live most of our lives in the conscious mind.

I was in my early forties when I fell ill with a condition called bipolar. I believed that this was brought on by being too nice and placing my trust in the answers of others. I would do anything for others; my biggest problem was that I could not say NO to people. I would often put myself out for others; this habit became so ingrained in me that it was impossible for me to say no. People and friends took huge advantage of my weakness, but what was happening to me was that my Wall of Doubt was building hugely between the two minds, my doubt was becoming super powerful against me; this was the main cause of my bipolar.

While building the Wall of Doubt, I noticed when you ask a person a question, they love to answer it. It's the feeling of importance that they are after, even if their answer to you only has partial truth. On the discovery of this, I made a rule to myself; any questions that I need answers to, I would seek professional advice. Remember, if I can teach you anything from this chapter, please let it be this: when seeking advice, ask only people who are qualified enough to give such advice, for it should only be professional advice that you use to build the new Doors to Success.

While lying in bed at night, my thoughts would often race; it was a horrible feeling. Thoughts from every story in my life, thoughts like outstanding bills, career, relationships and from my past. They would enter my mind and speed through the stories. I had no control over what thoughts came in or what stories I could revisit. These thought patterns would happen for long periods of time and I was exhausted; I never got much sleep. These patterns were compelling my bipolar. My emotions and feelings were flying up and down in seconds, the butterflies in my tummy were so intense and the sad depressed feelings of complete emptiness and loneliness were unbearable.

Here's how I broke through the Wall of Doubt:

One day I was telling my brother and son, whom I have an innovation business with, about the racing thoughts I was having. My brother said "Paddy, when the thoughts start racing, shout out loud in your own mind, 'STOP!'" The next time the racing thoughts showed up, I remembered the technique my brother told me, I used it and it worked, so I keep using it each time and now they are GONE, some years since.

Another discovery was brought to me by my son – exercising peace of mind. An exercise to prove to myself that I'm in control of my thoughts. When I go for a walk with my little dog I say to myself, "I'm going to clear my head from thoughts," so I can decide when. What I do is, I say to myself, "At this next street lamp, I'm not going to think about anything at all and I'm going to clear my thoughts until I reach the next street lamp." On my first attempt, it lasted two seconds, then I tried again and it was for five seconds, I thought that this was going to be impossible but I practiced and practiced, now I can tell you, it's a wonderful gift from God and the control and peace of mind is beautiful.

The last of the three things is, I sought only advice from competent professionals. I can't emphasize this enough; remember the answers from others built the Wall of Doubt. There is a God – anytime I want anything in my life, I ask the Universe and I always receive. Mind you, I do allow time to receive and funny as it may seem, it always comes back at the right moment.

The only thing holding you back from success is your Wall of Doubt, though most of you will disagree and tell me that it is others or outside circumstances that hold you back. Let me tell you when you try to achieve something new, your ego – the voice in your head – will make plenty of excuses as to why you will not be able to achieve the new idea; excuses like you don't have the money or the time, or you are not skilled enough. The ego lives in your stories in the Wall of Doubt between the two minds, the conscious mind, and the subconscious mind; the ego will give its life to hold you prisoner in the conscious mind. Its life, by the way, is the stories in the brickage-beliefs and the blockage-beliefs that lie in the Wall of Doubt. The reason you dwell in your past memories/stories is the work of your ego; the ego grows stronger when it has control over you.

How does the ego get stronger in you? Every time you try something new and fail, the Wall of Doubt grows stronger. The ego will say things to you like, I had a feeling that would not work, or you can try it again sometime. The ego knows you inside out and it works on your downfall; it is sly and slippery – it is clever – and it will try every trick in the book to defeat you. Here is a simple task for you to try, STOP THINKING, clear your mind of everything for twenty seconds; see how hard it is to do. The reason for that is the ego has built itself into the voice of your thoughts and pretends to be you talking to you. The one thing I did to take control of my ego was, I would say things to myself, things like I might try to do this new thing tomorrow or next week. My ego would not know which day I was going to try the new thing, so it could not set the plan for me to fail. Self-sabotage comes from the ego but when it doesn't know your plan it will fail to fail you. The ego is a part of you, but for most, it is larger than them. When you keep your plans to your true self, you will be successful, and every time you succeed the ego gets weaker. You should not aim to kill the ego just tame it, so it doesn't have the say in your plans.

Breaking through the Wall of Doubt can be tricky because the ego does not want to be the underdog. So start by taking out the brickage beliefs, the smaller beliefs in the Wall of Doubt. When you break through the Wall of Doubt, you will enter the subconscious mind where your spirit and abundance lie. Most people call this part of the mind the creative side, connected to God where all ideas come from.

Thank you for reading my chapter. I hope it was useful to you, and I look forward to assisting you sometime soon.

Patrick Hayden is a personal Life Mentor, a Life Coach with a difference, an Inventor and an International Best-Selling Author in the book *Living Without Limitations – 30 Mentors to Rock Your World*. His personal drive within his heart is to help others overcome their brickage and blockage beliefs and enhance their lives to the success they deserve. Married for twenty-eight years to his beautiful wife Cora, who has stood by him through thick and thin, Patrick has three wonderful sons and in June 2014, he became a grandfather. He now enjoys living life without limits.

Compiled by Anita Sechesky

CHAPTER TWENTY

Releasing to Begin Healing
by Luciel Greene

In this chapter, I am connecting you to the female energy and inner child, the nurturer, the giver, the emotional wreck, people pleasing, manipulated, and manipulating little girl.

The one who can throw a tantrum because she is feeling rejected, abandoned, unloved, and insecure.

Living many traumatic experiences that hurt frightened me physically and emotionally as well as spiritually.

At the age of three, my parents decided to move to Calgary. After a week of traveling, with the last stretch being the longest, my parents were exhausted, and I napped a good part of the time. Arriving at a strange house, I was curious and of course hungry.

My parents fell sound asleep. My brother, who was five years old at the time, was on the couch and carried his blanket everywhere, just like the character Linus in Charlie Brown.

I climbed on the stove top, turned on the element, and started putting spices on it. My nightgown caught fire and I jumped off, but the wind fed its flames as I started screaming and running all over the place. The flames kept rising until my mother woke up and wrapped my brother's comforter around me quickly to choke the flames.

My folks had no idea how to get me to the hospital safely. It was 1982 and there was no 911 or cell phones. I was dying and ended up with major scarlet fever and 3rd degree burns on my right upper leg. Finally, at the Emergency Department, they immersed me in a bath of ice water. Seeing my skin sagging and the smell of burned flesh, I was in shock and would fall in and out of consciousness.

Hospitalized for 2 ½ months after a major surgery, I missed my parents. Realistically they couldn't be there 24/7. That's where my sociable nature came. I remember going into patients rooms to play cards, which was driving the nurses crazy because I was never in my room. One day they put a safety net over my crib so I wouldn't run away. When my Dad showed up, he started freaking on the staff and said, "She's not an animal!" A four-year-old boy in the same room as me never had visitors. My mother felt bad as he would cry and reach his arms out for my mama to hold him. I would get upset and jealous that he was taking her attention which I needed. That's where my first trigger of insecurity came.

Eight months after the incident, when I was four, I was playing out on the side of my triplex apartment with the grey flat bugs that are under the rocks. I remembered playing with a little girl from next door the day before. I knocked on the wrong neighbor's door because I thought my friend lived there. Two men kept me against my will. They made me urinate in a cup because I wanted to leave and tried to use the bathroom as an excuse. One man had me sitting on his bed, scared. I remember he was in his underwear playing the guitar and sent his roommate to get me peanuts at the store. My mom, who was only 4' 11" and 95 pounds, was looking for me everywhere. The one man at first denied I was there, but by then she heard me scream, "MOM!" She charged in there like a bull and grabbed me to save the day. This incident was kept hidden in my memories as a taboo. I felt like it was my fault because I never should've knocked on that door in the first place. I felt ashamed and mad at my dad. I wanted him to beat that neighbor up to save the day, but again it's my mom who rescued me. My dad worked a lot and he was raised in a family where he was considered the black sheep by my grandpa, so he didn't really know how to be an attentive dad.

Thirty-five years later, I had a flashback of the peanuts. It was triggered by someone who had bought a huge bag and offered me some. Strange how certain smells or items can remanifest horror in a split second. Has this happened to you? I especially thought I had healed that part of myself and so I decided to confront my inner demons to leave my little girl alone.

My Journey Unfolded

Growing up in a lower income project had no importance to me. I felt naïve and innocent. I simply wanted to make friends and make people happy. I was a social butterfly who wanted attention and love. I would play, but a lot of times, I felt there were older kids that wanted to play in ways that hurt and raped my innocence.

Looking back on it, I can't believe our parents let us roam around with no supervision.

At the age of ten, I was taking public transportation and had to transfer between two buses that would take me to school and back. Another problem arose: there was a fifteen-year-old girl who thought it would be okay to pick on little me. Every day, no matter what route or stop I took, she was there, like my worst nightmare. I started smoking at that age because I didn't want her to beat me up so I would do what she asked. Every day was a bad dream. She slapped me around until one day my when parents weren't home, she started pounding on my patio door. I got scared and called 911. The police showed up but couldn't find her anywhere. As soon as they left, she was right back at the door. I don't know why but I was outside, she grabbed me by the hair and bashed my forehead on the bumper of a car about fifteen times. After a few months of this terror, my mother chased her and told her to leave me alone. We moved away to a safer place, but was it really any safer?

I lost my virginity at the age of thirteen. I made him wait six months, but then he ruined my reputation at school. At thirteen years of age, I was cursed with 36 DDD Cup. When I was fourteen, I had a breast reduction because I was constantly sexually harassed at school. Can you recall as a teenager how difficult it was? What can you remember that wasn't so pleasant?

From the beginning of my teenage years, it wasn't too encouraging. At sixteen, I was being stalked by a taxi driver at school and a friend of mine had just been murdered because of a street gang. Fear was definitely in the air and for three months, the taxi driver watched my every move when I was on break. One day as I was leaving a friend's place to go home, I was walking to my bus stop when another man passed by very slowly and gave me the creeps. There was something about his look that petrified me. As I got to the bus stop, he had driven a block to meet me at that corner. He must have driven fast! He tried to lure me into his truck, but I said no thanks. Then he got out and said, "Get in the @#$%^^& truck!" I was paralyzed and couldn't move. If the bus hadn't shown up then, God knows what could have happened. I went to the police station because I had enough of this intimidation. I actually filed two harassment complaints, one for the taxi driver and the second for the psycho at the bus stop. The first question the police asked me was, "What were you wearing?" I was so upset because that day I was wearing a thick white sweater and clean jeans. I then felt again like I caused this because I looked too sexy. A private investigator came to the school, then went to see the cab driver and told him that if he ever stopped in front of the school again or so much as looked at me, he would go to jail. By then I started putting on pounds and to this day, I am now 222 lbs. After a lot of reflection, my weight was a form of protection from predators. I learned how to accept my feminine and inner child energy. A good balancing is in order to function at my best.

Co-dependency ended up being one of my problems with all my relationships because again, I was in my people pleasing, desperately trying to hold on to the idea of being in the perfect relationship. What a challenge and disappointment!

Can you relate or know someone who is like this?

I am grateful for my lessons and all the wonderful miracles including being alive, having the tools I need to continue my journey and to share with you some of my personal stories. I am a spiritual being living the human experience. I am here to resolve my karmic debts from previous lifetimes as well as this one. I am here to make peace with my heart and soul, and secure my inner child by learning to forgive and receive forgiveness. My mission is to help others who have gone through painful experiences.

Learning to say NO when things aren't okay was a hard learning curve. Staying in unhealthy relationships to hang on to the good times isn't enough to hold me there anymore. Even if I paint the perfect relationship, it doesn't turn out to be what I expect. I have moved twelve times with four different partners in the period of sixteen years. Let me tell you that it's not easy when you try to provide a good stable life for three children with ADHD and my diagnosis of Multiple Sclerosis.

Every time I thought I had found the partner of a lifetime, the switch came. My kids took up so much of my time and energy, with their fighting constantly. It brought me to realize that starting over with another partner is not my answer. The solution sits in my heart and soul. Honestly, all I need to do is give my kids and I the love we deserve, and then I think the rest will follow.

I clearly understand now that I can forgive, let go of fear, and move on to new and wonderful experiences that will lead to my highest good and vibrate positivity. I realize that I need to nurture that little girl inside because when I feel abandoned or rejected, she takes up a lot of space. I learned to listen to her so that I can get through whatever it is I need to deal with. Also, I will never give up on my kids no matter who comes my way.

I have learned to become my own parent. Transformation came with time, life experiences, and therapy. Sometimes the best therapy for me was talking to a friend or going out in nature. I can connect by taking a walk in the forest, stopping to smell the flowers, and giving myself extra love by doing things I enjoy.

My creative outlet is art as it nourishes my soul and inner child. I started writing a lot of what was going on in my life from a very young age. It was a form of release for me. Painting also helps bring out the fantastic world of faeries and angels that guide me every step of the way. Archangel Michael is there to cut negative cords and shield me from harm. I picture a blue or white bubble shielding me. It helps keep dark energies away from me.

I have my karma and I need to learn from living the experiences. Once the lesson is learned, my energy shifts and I change as well. If the lesson is not learned the first time, it will continue to come bite me in the butt until I get it right.

Parents are supposed to be there to protect their children. However, sometimes even if one tries, they cannot save us all the time from dark souls.

Luciel Greene was born in Ottawa, Ontario. She is the mother of three children and proud owner of Luciel's Divine Connections. She is a Medium, helps those in need, practices Intuitive healing and energetic cleansings, is a certified Tao Healing Hands soul healer, certified Reiki Practitioner, painter, author, and poet. Luciel believes we are all spiritual beings living a human experience to solve our karmic debts. She transformed from being a people pleaser and living poisonous relationships to choosing self-love. Luciel connected to her heaven's team and sees things through a different eye, one that is deep in her core.

More Stories to Heal Your World Now

Compiled by Anita Sechesky

CHAPTER TWENTY-ONE

MORE Healing for the Spirit
by Anita Sechesky

The human spirit is so magnificent. It is the connection to the human mind and body and has the capacity to connect with other human beings. We can almost feel the emotional pain or trauma another person has lived through. I believe that love is such a powerful energy that gives us hope and causes our spirits to become connected as one. I am a strong believer that our spirits live forever.

For this chapter, I would like to share my own personal experience when I had lost my first child. My daughter was full-term, and she was a perfect baby. There was nothing wrong the entire pregnancy. However, we did lose our beautiful little girl due to unforeseen causes. I had known something was not right and felt it within my spirit. I asked my doctor if I could be induced to have my daughter delivered two weeks early. My Obstetrician's office was over two hours away from my hometown. He decided not to interfere with the natural birth process that was planned since there wasn't any cause for concern at this point. When I went to the Emergency Department in my small hometown, I was always told by the nurses that everything was fine and even though my baby's heart rate was lower as compared to earlier assessments in my pregnancy. This occurred before I became a Registered Nurse and disturbed me as I already had some medical knowledge at the time.

My pregnancy loss with my daughter was the most heartbreaking thing I have endured. No one from the hospital offered any support. Sadly, the loss of my baby was not the first one in this community. I tried to tell the nurses so many times that something was not right, but no one took me seriously. I must have gone to the Emergency Department at least a dozen times and was always told that I was overreacting or something to that extent. The last time I went to Emerg, they staff finally took me seriously and put a stress monitor on me. All the previous times I went in, the stress monitor was already being used or I was just sent home. I wasn't even given the option to wait for the monitor to confirm my concerns.

As it turned out, my precious baby girl was stillborn and I had to deliver her on a maternity ward during the Christmas holidays just two days before my own birthday. It was painful to see the other mothers and their live babies. The night before my induction, my daughter's little baby spirit came to me and before I knew it, I was hovering above my body looking down at my husband lying next to my lifeless body. I saw how my hands were folded across my pregnant belly with my daughter still within my womb. I remember looking at how beautiful and bright she was and then, just like that, I got caught up in the instantaneous rapture of leaving my physical body. Then as I was traveling upwards into the heavenly realms with my daughter, I remembered what my mom had just moments earlier spoken to me about and I looked back down at my husband sleeping. She said that I should remember how much he loved me and that we would have more children one day. The very moment that thought flashed through my mind, I was back inside my physical body and looking at my hands folded in front of me.

This experience left me realizing that death is only a transition and not a physical effort at all. In fact, my experience was completely effortless and merely a shift out of my physical body into my spiritual body. I believe that we already have our spiritual bodies inside of us and when we no longer need our physical bodies, we simply leave them behind. However, you may want to analyze it, I know it was a profound and powerful revelation that gave me confirmation of life after death. How amazing to know that we never actually die or lose ourselves, but we are intact in our thoughts even after our physical bodies stop working! This is the reason I am a strong believer in my Christian faith. I am confidently hopeful that I will be reunited with my loved ones and even embrace my baby girl once more in my arms.

I have learned that our spirit man is the essence of who we are. This perception is so profound that it can help us to become stronger in this life if we allow ourselves to accept that nothing is impossible and that all is possible if we believe.

Yes, the human spirit is powerful and I can even tell you an experience I had when our dear family pet died. It was a hard time for all of us as our doggie girl was part of our family for over thirteen years. She was like our first child and was well loved within our community by our friends and family. I will never forget that following the first Mother's Day service after we had lost our daughter, our pet doggie came into the bedroom and looked at me crying as I was curled up on my bed. She jumped up and snuggled right against my belly, as if someone had coaxed her to do that. She stayed there for a moment, jumped down, looked at me, and then walked away. When our beloved pet passed away at my parent's home, it was devastating because we never had a chance to say good-bye to her. The following day, I was sitting in my glider rocking chair just thinking that I never had a chance to tell her how much I loved her. All of a sudden, out of nowhere, I literally felt this amazing rush of energy. It was like a swift breeze. Before I knew it, our dog in her spiritual form was sitting right next to me by my feet. Then automatically I felt my Spirit man lean down, pat her, and even say, "Good girl." I couldn't believe this was happening and excitedly told my husband that I got to say goodbye to our pet. He was so happy and never doubted me because of the supernatural experiences I already had.

My reason for sharing these events is to help you realize that our spirit is something that every living person has within. There is no explaining it. I believe from the time our cells are conceived and start vibrating, we are created out of pure love and positive energy as we are all perfect creations by God within this Universe and all its glory. There is no need to fear the fact that our spirit is something that is unexplained. In fact, I believe in some special way if we embrace our lives differently, we may be exposed to more infinite possibilities that we would never have realized were always around us anyways. Many people already know that God is a spirit that we cannot see, yet those same individuals believe He exists around us. Be open-minded to what our Creator has created within you. You are unique and wonderfully made. Never doubt the endless possibilities of your human spirit. This life is but a journey and we are all headed in the same direction.

We don't have to personally know each other to understand life's hardships, trauma, and pain. Our unity as individuals simply believing in the common good creates a connection within our spirits. Can you imagine so many people across the globe equally realizing the need to reach out and show more empathy, compassion, and love for those around them? The human spirit ignited in love will unite many. God is Love and God is Hope. Have you connected with Him yet? It's all about relationship, not rituals. Just like any other relationship, start with introducing yourself. He accepts you just as you are. Maybe it's time you do the same. Healing will become one of the benefits from this relationship. It all starts with you wanting more for yourself. The human spirit is one of the most beautiful gifts we have been given. It has unlimited possibilities.

Many times, we may face extreme difficulties in our lives. When hopelessness feels like it is prevailing, what do you do? Do you have a support system? Not everyone does, which is a sad reality in this big world. Lives are changed instantly because of either good or bad experiences. When you carry pain deep within your heart, it affects the vibrancy of your life. Maybe it's time to start associating with positive hopeful people. Discover what your life's passions are by searching deep within your soul. You can begin your own healing right now, right where you are.

Anita Sechesky

Anita is the Brampton Chapter President of the Holistic Chamber of Commerce because she believes in supporting all entrepreneurs who work from a mind, body & spirit perspective. As a Registered Nurse with over twenty years in Health Care, she has worked with all age groups and diversities.

Anita has excellent written, and communication skills is empathetic and goal-oriented. She is as an ICF - Certified Professional Coach, Publisher, Law of Attraction Practitioner, and soon-to-be Master of NLP Practitioner, as well as a #1 and multiple Best-Selling author.

Email: **lwlclienthelp@gmail.com**

Website: **www.lwlpublishinghouse.com**

Compiled by Anita Sechesky

WORDS OF ENCOURAGEMENT

Life is full of beauty and grace. When it becomes dark and scary, we have the strength, courage, and conviction to brighten the dreary with brilliant light. Keep an attitude of gratitude and know that you are in control of how it comes about. Open the windows to light ...and free your spirit!

MARY HILTY

More Stories to Heal Your World Now

CHAPTER TWENTY-TWO

The Power of Words
by Natalie Bélair

I never imagined that my path was heading the way of an International Best-Selling Author.

All my life, I struggled with sharing my experiences, thoughts, feelings, and words. I can remember to this day growing up feeling nervous and anxious about standing in front of the classroom or a conference as a speaker. I get so nervous that my ears and chest area turn as red as a hot tomato and I want to throw up.

I dreaded presentations at school. My teachers always started alphabetically with our last names. Oh man, I felt cursed. My last name being "Bélair" meant I was always the first to present. I wondered what people thought and judged myself as I wanted to say and share the perfect words.

Growing up, I was always told that kids did not have a place at the table with the adults. If I sat with them, I needed to be quiet. That was hard for me; I always had an opinion to share.

I quickly learned to ignore my emotions and thoughts until they no longer existed. I felt like it was taboo for me to have a daily conversation with my parents about my day.

Then came the weekly dictations and daily journaling. Whew... not so easy for me!

The struggles of sharing what I had suppressed deep within would never seem to find its way on paper. I no longer knew how to communicate; I found myself, filled with excuses, running away from all assignments.

I studied hard and tried my best, however it was never enough. One dictation after another, pages were covered in red markings every single week, from elementary to high school.

As my struggles with writing continued, my 10th-grade teacher, Mr. P., once told me that, "You will never amount to anything, nor go anywhere in life as you do not know how to write." My eyes fill up with tears as I take this opportunity to share my feelings of being discouraged and disappointed.

A flashback to when I was seventeen and my father told me, "Natalie, you don't need to learn Spanish as you will never go anywhere in life!" Drenched in sadness, I embrace this moment. My emotions do not define me!

I choose to use my most powerful tool, *my present emotions*, to serve as a roadblock destroyer. It's my force deep within to move forward with my mission.

I can't change what they said. However, I can control my reaction by choosing to be responsible for how it affects me.

Throughout my soul journey, I always wanted to run away from any lessons and courses that required writing exercises. If journaling or writing was involved, I either denied myself taking the course or I would find another way around it, like suggest therapy sessions as it was important for me to flourish.

Oddly enough, I became accustomed to speaking based on my constant presentations growing up. For the longest time, I seriously thought that my mission was to serve by sharing my stories and grounded truth as a speaker. Nope! Not at all, as I chuckle to myself. *The Divine always has a bigger plan!* I am not in control. I thought I was, but Divine and God will laugh.

One day, following my guidance, I took a leap of faith and plunged into a two-year living in relations course that involved speaking, listening, writing, and understanding about my thoughts and emotions in my current life experiences and my childhood.

I found my way through all the teachings and exercises except for writing. Wow...did I ever have resistance to writing! I found every excuse in the book to avoid it. My unconscious mind had other expectations. I pleaded with the teacher as to why it was so important for me not do the writing exercises – I was meant to be a speaker and not a writer. Therefore, I would do a therapy session after each class for two years and verbally discuss my work instead, I pleaded.

I never noticed that I was actually blocked and not doing myself a favor. I persisted and continued to defend myself as to why I didn't want to write in my therapy sessions. Until one day!

Face to face with my therapist, I started to cry as I saw a vision. The piece of paper that I was holding in my hands turned red and full of blood with the feelings of hurt, pain, and failure. Frozen there at that moment, I heard the playback of Mr. P's and my father's words "that you will not go anywhere." I was faced with my judgments of fear of failure and success.

I choose to give myself the love and acknowledgment I deserve. As I embraced that awakening of my AHA moment with unconditional love, my paper slowly turned from blood red to a lovely soft pink as it filled with love, appreciation, and gratitude for profound healing. Grounded in my truth, I AM capable of expressing my heartfelt experience on paper.

I AM perfect in my imperfections!

The underlining gift within was that I was truly afraid to write my truth on paper as it made it real. I was neglecting the reality by not taking responsibility and owning it.

I AM THAT I AM!

I speak, write, and feel my truth! Spelling mistakes and all, I love myself unconditionally. That's why the world has editors, right?

I am grateful for the editors along my path as I no longer have to live in the fear of failure or success. I will no longer stop myself from following my heart and soul journey. That's how I live my life without limitations, beloved souls.

In closing, I would like to give my gratitude to my heaven's team, all the teachers along my journey, countless bow downs to the Divine with continuous love and gratitude flowing to all.

I am forever grateful!

Love & Light

Natalie Bélair was born and raised in Timmins, Ontario and currently lives in Ottawa. She is an International Best-Selling Author and Owner of Angelic Changes. Natalie is a Certified Intuitive Energy & Soul Healer, Spiritual Teacher, Soul Communicator, Inspirational Speaker, and Road Block Destroyer with over eighteen years' experience in medical management. She uses a heart-centered "Soul Song" to remove soul, mind, emotional, and body blockages to transform all aspects of life, both in the present and past lifetimes. Her mission is to be an Unconditional Servant, spreading love, peace, harmony and to shine her light as brightly as possible.

Facebook: **www.facebook.com/IntuitiveEnergySoulHealing**

Website: **http://angelicchanges.com/**

Compiled by Anita Sechesky

CHAPTER TWENTY-THREE

I Will Never Forget Her Last Words to Me
by Anita Sechesky

For as long as I can remember, I always had a unique perspective on life. There were even times that I felt as though no one liked or appreciated me. Many times over growing up, I recall my mom telling me not to think like that. My dear sweet mom has always been my voice of reason. When I got offended or hurt by the remarks or attitudes of others, she always told me to forgive them. Thank you, Mom but I still had to figure them out.

I could never figure out why people behaved the way they did, which is probably why I became a Registered Nurse and now a Certified Professional Coach. I love to analyze and understand others. One of my most disturbing discoveries was realizing how so many people who were mean or negative towards me were actually jealous. This was confirmed to me by a distant relative who is a well-known minister and counselor to many in New York City. He confided in me based on what he knew already, and what God had revealed to him that there were many individuals very close to me who were indeed jealous and I should be wary of their motives. What a confirmation and eye-opener at that time.

So many things in my life started to make sense. I now understood the snide remarks, such as "Not everyone could be a nurse," or "I don't care if you are a nurse ..." How could people so close to me be so cruel and heartless? How would they feel if someone said that to their own loved one? Little do they realize how much hatred, mental, and verbal abuse I had already endured during my 1st year of training in Nursing School. The instructors, whom I once had such high regard for, were initially pleasant and supportive of me as an eager student, let me down. They did a complete switch in their response towards me during my 2nd year of training. For unknown reasons, they changed their attitudes and behaviors towards me even after I had successfully completed the whole 1st year with a perfect GPA of 4.0. What an accomplishment considering the curriculum was part of a very prestigious university. Although I was the only non-white student in my class, I have always chosen to look past these visible differences. My grades could not be disputed considering the time and effort I put into my education. Based on the events that occurred at that time in my life, I can tell you that I would have never imagined in a million years people who call themselves caring professionals could be as cruel and heartless as these women were towards me. The most significant lesson I learned was that the human mind, will, and emotions play an intricate role in helping the human spirit to persevere when all hope is stolen and damaged. I am so thankful that I never committed suicide when I was in the pit of despair, feeling worn out, and struggling to survive. It was at that moment I cried out to God, asking HIM that if HE wanted me to be a nurse, it had to be for more than just me. There must be a bigger plan, and if HE wanted me to survive this living nightmare, HE would make a way when there seemed to be no way. God has proven to me that HE doesn't make junk.

Another one of the most trying and challenging times of my life was when I received a phone call in the middle of the night that my late Grandma had been taken to the Emergency Department and wasn't doing good. I recall watching my Grandma as she declined in health after being admitted to the hospital ward where I worked. It was my home floor where I started my first full-time position as an RN. I was hired as a Cardiology Nurse. Through those years, I developed some wonderful friendships, and one of my colleagues had become the Nurse Manager on the floor. When my Grandma was admitted to the hospital, she had suffered multiple injuries, leaving her broken and blind in one eye. As you can imagine, it was horrific to see her in this condition. I picked up as many shifts as I could, even though I just found out that I was pregnant with my second child. Now because of the unexpected stress and emotional abuse I endured during my Grandma's hospitalization from people very close to me, I was at risk of my pregnancy being terminated. My doctor scheduled weekly ultrasounds to keep track of my baby's growth and development. My Grandma never fully recovered from her injuries.

But I will never forget the last words she ever said to me from her hospital bed. I had just completed my shift, and this was when I could spend time alone with her without any interruptions. This particular night I was crying as I sat next to her. She said to me "Bae, why are you crying?" I told her "They don't like me." My Grandma then said "They don't like me either. But Jesus loves me and HE loves you and I love you too." These words are so powerful. They have more meaning than a thousand words can say.

My dear sweet deceased Grandma lived a life that is a legacy to what one person can accomplish on her own. She was a widow at twenty-eight years of age with eight children to raise on her own. She has inspired me to realize that we don't need the praise and worship of others. We must first believe in ourselves. My Grandma loved and respected everyone for who they were. She accepted each person she met in her life, never judged others, but always believed that everyone including her grandchildren and great-grandchildren deserved to be all that they were created to be. She was proud of every one of them and always tried to maintain peace and unity among her family. Her greatest desire was that all her children would come to understand the relationship she had with her Heavenly Father. Grandma's faith had brought her through some of the worst things she experienced in her lifetime. I am sure there were many that even my dad and his sibling did not know about. After all, life could not have been easy being a single mother in the 1940's and 1950's with no formal education and support of family. Yet my grandma managed to raise and educate and professionally train all of her children so they could support their own families one day. What a woman! I am so proud of the legacy she has left behind and to have known and loved her.

When my son was born I named him in honor of his late great-grandma and one day when he is older, I will tell him of the amazing woman she was and her dream and vision for her loved ones. We can all do our part. It starts within our hearts to show others what we are made of and where we originate from.

I guess this is why I am who I am with a determined grandma who never gave up on her goals in life. It must be part of my DNA. Thank you, Dad. A mother's love continues to carry through the generations. My parents have instilled in me that it is not my problem what others think of me. Instead, it becomes my problem if I choose to think less of myself.

I want to encourage you never to give up whether it is a dream, ambition, or lifelong goal. You deserve the right to have the opportunity to prove to yourself that you are more than capable. Don't listen to the lies of others. God created you perfect in HIS image. You were born for greatness. Step into the life that is waiting for you.

Maybe you lost someone dear to you, and you felt like you had no control over the circumstances to even be part of their life. I know I could have helped to make my grandma more comfortable by caring for her and giving her my love. But, the choice was not given to me even though I represented my dad as his eldest child. I always try to help others have a good life. Every human being deserves to leave this world in dignity, comfort, and pain-free. As nurses, we see many things. But the hardest is to be completely helpless when it's your loved ones.

If you are still struggling with a loss, allow yourself time to grieve and forgive what needs to be forgiven. We cannot change the past; we can only learn from it. In this life one thing can be sure; we will all come to the end of our journeys one day. What you allow for others should be exactly what you would allow for yourselves.

Anita Sechesky

Anita is the Brampton Chapter President of the Holistic Chamber of Commerce because she believes in supporting all entrepreneurs who work from a mind, body & spirit perspective. As a Registered Nurse with over twenty years in Health Care, she has worked with all age groups and diversities.

Anita has excellent written, and communication skills is empathetic and goal-oriented. She is as an ICF - Certified Professional Coach, Publisher, Law of Attraction Practitioner, and soon-to-be Master of NLP Practitioner, as well as a #1 and multiple Best-Selling author.

Email: **lwlclienthelp@gmail.com**

Website: **www.lwlpublishinghouse.com**

Compiled by Anita Sechesky

CHAPTER TWENTY-FOUR

I Never Got a Chance to Say Goodbye

by Valentina Gjorgjievski

I had the unfortunate experience at the age of twenty-five of going through a traumatic event by losing my father to a sudden and unexpected heart attack, and my world was suddenly turned upside down. I recall it being three years to the day in March 2014; it was a dark and stormy Saturday night in my hometown of Sydney, Australia. I was just finishing my studies for Semester 1 for my first psychology assignment for the year, and I remember getting ready go out for the night but having this horrible feeling that I shouldn't be going anywhere. The feeling was intense, but I pushed it aside thinking that I was just being silly; only at that very moment my younger sister walked through my bedroom door and voiced the same concerns. We both felt it but didn't know what it was. She tried to convince me not to go out, but my friend whom I had made plans with would not take no for an answer. I tried desperately to cancel my plans to no avail.

Leaving my bedroom to go to the kitchen where the rest of the family was, I noticed that nothing seemed amiss. Mum was washing the dishes, and my brother was standing at the bench talking to her. Dad was sitting at the dining table playing with his music mixer, his headphones on, to get music ready for his upcoming tour at the end of the year, which was a daily thing for him. Nothing was out of place. Deciding against my inner intuition, I advised everyone in the room that I was leaving. As I turned to leave the kitchen something made me look at my father. He had no idea what was being said, as he did not remove his headphones from his ears, but he made eye contact with me indicating he knew I was going out. Not saying goodbye, I walked out the front door and into my friend's car against my better judgment.

Standing in the middle of a crowded nightclub, I looked at my phone which said it was almost 12 a.m. A few moments later I received a text message from my sister to come back home, that Dad had stopped breathing. Shock and panic overtook me as we sped in the car back home only to be too late; he was already on his way to the hospital, and it didn't look good. By exactly 12 a.m. that night, he was pronounced dead.

I never got a chance to say goodbye.

Over the course of the 2 ½ years since his death, I had changed in character and gone off track of who I was, but I was trying to find my way back. I found that being around other people made me feel better than sitting at home, and I surrounded myself with company from anyone who wanted to be around me at this very hard time without realizing they weren't the right people to be around. I had blocked out the memory of that fateful night and the events following, although I remembered everything about my father during his life. If my friends started talking about death, I would either leave the room or would distract myself to not listen to the conversation. It was too traumatic for me.

I experienced sharp pains in my chest, similar to a heart attack sensation for almost twelve months. My friends noticed that I started to withdraw and I was no longer interested in the things that we used to do or talk about. I developed a weaker version of my character for the course of two years that people took advantage of. I did not have the energy to defend myself, and I became overly sensitive. Being known as the brains of the family, it was a shock to everyone that I could no longer think straight. I didn't realize it, but there was a change in the dynamics of my relationship with my mother. She was going through her own grieving process, but I became very overprotective of her constantly, like I was the parent. I wouldn't let her out of my sight, because I feared of losing her the same way.

My connection and bond with my father was a very close and strong one, being that we were a very close and happy family. I grew up in a happy home and had the best of everything, which made his death even harder, especially knowing what his plans were for the future. As time goes on, memories will also trigger these emotions. Being that he was a musician, quiet was not a normal day in our household. We were taught that life is music. An average day for us at home was five different types of live music blaring from five different corners of the house all at the same time. Quiet did not exist in our household. But when he passed away, due to religious beliefs, the house was quiet.

Just weeks before he passed away he sat me down as if knowing what was going to happen and told me what he wanted me to do and to listen to him and no one else. This kept repeating itself in my mind and kept me going throughout the whole ordeal. My strength of character also assisted me to keep going – I was the strongest in the family. I overcame not only my own grief and despair but also carried my mother, brother, and sister to overcome their own.

The recovery process has taken almost three years and is still continuing as there is no time limit to grief. I was very close to my Dad and surviving his death was not an easy journey. The connection between my Dad and me has not been broken in spirit, and I will always be daddy's little girl.

"You'll always be in my heart. In loving memory

To my Dad" Love,

Tina

In my career, I had assisted many clients in overcoming trauma and grief. But it wasn't until I went through it myself that I actually fully understood what they went through. I found that a lot of people don't understand what it is like to lose someone close to you, and how the mind reacts and copes. I found myself saying to a lot of people that they didn't understand, a statement that I also hear from a lot of my clients.

So how did I survive this very traumatic event in my life?

- My strength of character
- My bond with my immediate family – my mother, brother and sister
- Holding on to Dad's last words to me and my memories of him
- I appreciated what he valued in his life that made him unique, such as his music
- His quirky sense of humor and his strange musical habits
- The values that he taught me and the things that he encouraged me to do

If you have lost someone close to you, you may want to write a memory list to help you overcome your loss.

Grieving is not a mental illness, even though you may show signs of post-traumatic stress disorder. Each person goes through their own experience of grief and loss; it is not the same across the board, it's an individual experience. You may experience several of the following: physical distress such as chest pains, change in appetite, weight change, crying, feelings of emptiness, extreme anger, irritability, guilt, loneliness, vulnerability, feelings of abandonment, being overly sensitive, dependence on others, being withdrawn, avoiding other people, lack of interest in things and people, forgetfulness, searching for the deceased, not thinking clearly, trying not to talk about death and needing to retell the story.

Here are some things to remember and incorporate into your daily routine while going through these stages. Do not compare your experience to someone else's – everyone mourns and reacts differently. Talk to others that you can trust but be careful whom you trust – there are many people out there who have not experienced losing someone and do not understand what you are going through, possibly deterring you in your recovery process. Introduce pleasant changes in your life; make plans to assist you to survive the weekends. It may be difficult to be motivated to go out, but it is very important in order for your mind to stay clear that you do not confine yourself to home. Understand that any feelings that you are going through are the normal grief reaction; until you are out of the grieving stages do not make any major life decisions. Do not listen to other people if they pressure you in any way – listen to yourself; you best know how you feel. Do things that you enjoy and that bring you happiness; be around positive people, do not sit alone during this time.

Compiled by Anita Sechesky

Valentina Gjorgjievska was born in Wollongong, Australia in 1985. She's had a successful career in the community services sector, helping many people to overcome their barriers and assisting them to re-enter the workforce, before becoming a writer. Valentina is now an International Best-Selling Author by co-authoring in her first three books: Living Without Limitations – 30 Stories to Heal Your World, Family Ties – What Binds Us and Tears Us Apart and Manifesting A New Life. She has completed courses in psychology and counseling and has a First Aid in Mental Health. Valentina is passionate about music, reading, and novel writing, and sang professionally in her younger years.

Skype: **valentinagjorgjievska**

Email: **valgjorgjievska1985@gmail.com**

Facebook: **facebook.com/valentina23**

Facebook: **facebook.com/valentina.gjorgjievska.92**

Twitter: **@valentinagj23**

LinkedIn: **linkedin.com/pub/valentina-gjorgjievska/87/4b7/2b7**

Compiled by Anita Sechesky

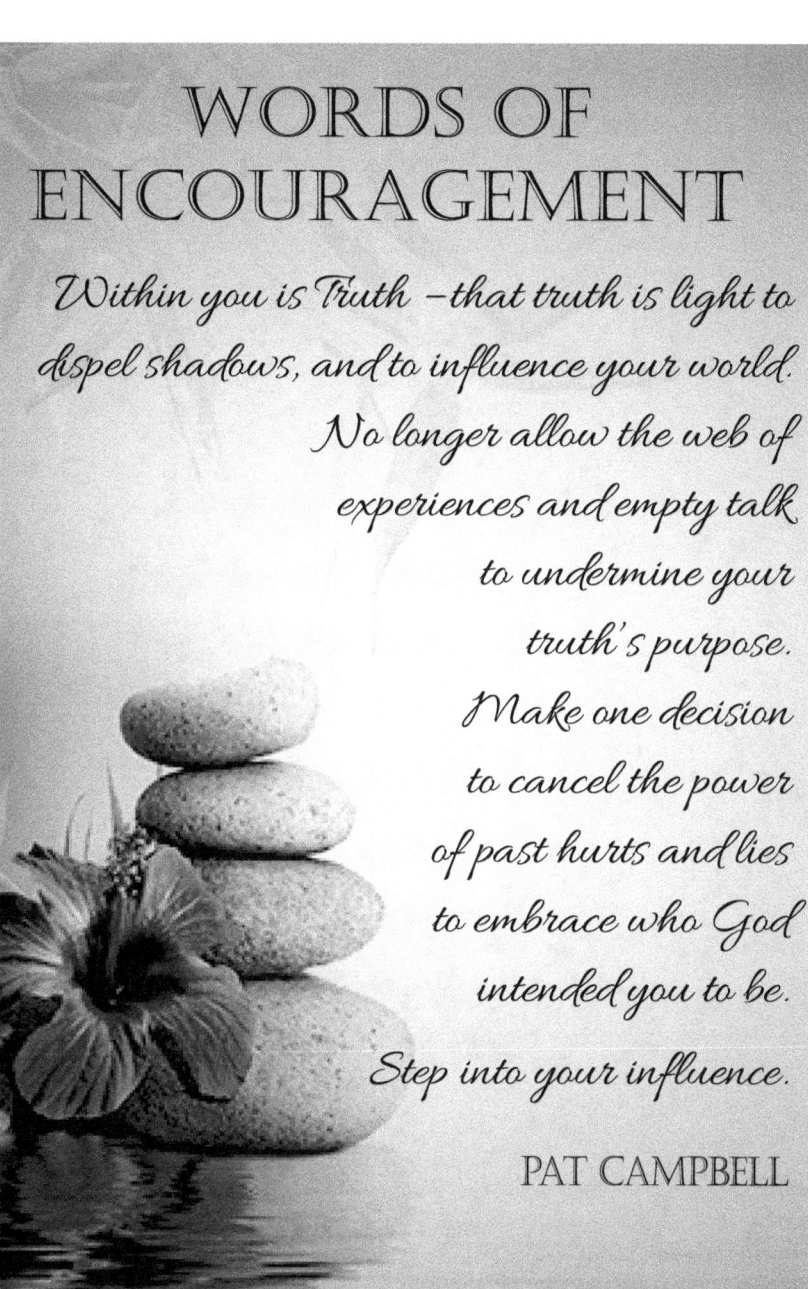

WORDS OF ENCOURAGEMENT

Within you is Truth – that truth is light to dispel shadows, and to influence your world. No longer allow the web of experiences and empty talk to undermine your truth's purpose. Make one decision to cancel the power of past hurts and lies to embrace who God intended you to be. Step into your influence.

PAT CAMPBELL

CHAPTER TWENTY-FIVE

The Crossroads to My Healing
by Gloria Delvecchio Callan

You have all heard the following expression many times before; live your life with "childlike faith." I remember feeling as a child that nothing was impossible and dreaming I could accomplish anything I set my mind to do. I believed, and I saw everyone through rose-colored lenses.

In my childhood, I had parents who were very different. My dad was a very handsome man who smiled all the time and loved everyone he met. He constantly told me that he loved me and encouraged me to chase all my dreams and that nothing was impossible to learn and achieve. Yet he had a personal problem with drinking. On the other hand, my mom was a disciplinarian; she never told me she loved me but had high expectations and demanded perfection. That was okay because I loved my parents so much and wanted to please them. Therefore, I excelled at everything – academics, sports, and relationships. My reasoning was that I wanted them to be proud of me.

When I was in high school, my parents were constantly fighting, and I was desperate to get away from the fighting at home. I traveled by bus every day for four years and to attend a small church chapel inside a hospital across the street from my high school. I believed there was something peaceful inside this place. This was a pivotal time in my life that would later prove to be a life preserver.

After high school, I wanted to follow my heart and decided on a nursing career to help people who were in need. Unfortunately, I finished school at an early age and this dream was put on hold. As my parents grew further apart, I had no direction or mentors to guide me in life. I met a man that was nine years older than me, whom I believed was going to give me a chance to have all I ever needed – children, a stable home and a way to fill the void in my heart. We faced many bumps in the road and surprises as we attempted to achieve a successful marriage and a stable life together.

Now, let us fast forward to four years later. We had two children, a girl and a boy whom I dearly loved. All was going according to plan, and my dream of having my own family was realized. Not so fast. My dad passed away from cancer; he was only 52. I was devastated and overwhelmed with grief. I never processed my grief for him, and my life felt like a car that was stuck in a ditch spinning and getting nowhere.

Now the ruts in the ditch got worse and I found myself pregnant with a third child in the winter after my dad passed away. My husband did not want another child and I was filled with tremendous anxiety at the prospect of having another child. At the time I was only twenty-one and my children were ages two and one. My husband was starting down a path of excessive drinking. To make matters worse, he told me, "I really did not want any children." The decision which I made changed the course of my life forever. Yes! I made the decision to abort this pregnancy. This did not come easily; I was scared, with no one to talk to, since abortion was not an issue talked about in the seventies. I would look at my children, the joy they brought to my life every day and would ask myself, "How can you think of an abortion?" Tears would just roll down my face like floodwaters.

As the days drifted by, I was taking care of my children with no participation from my husband. My mother was always criticizing me about how I raised my children. I was sinking like quicksand, and I had no one to turn to. I made all the arrangements for the abortion. I found a babysitter for the children and traveled to the United States by myself in the middle of winter to have this miserable procedure done in a small dingy clinic. The doctor explained that they would use a suction procedure and it would be all be over in thirty minutes, and I would be able to go home in two hours.

The nurses were cold as they were doing their duties as if it were a menial task like washing dishes – no compassion, no caring. The moments after the procedure left a hole in my heart like a tornado ripping it into million pieces, because I overheard the nurses say that the child was a boy!

I came home bleeding from the procedure; I was numb and felt ice cold like I had died but was still alive. It was surreal. I cared for my two children over the next days, months and years with love and cherished every moment with them. Yet my heart ached always for the child I lost, and I would become depressed or get very ill every year at the time my son would have been born. I was so bruised from this event that led to many crossroads in my life. It made me bitter, angry, depressed, jealous, selfish, unforgiving towards others, and determined that I was going to live a life of "doing it my way." I had lost my childlike faith and became very critical and judgmental. This contributed to feelings of unworthiness, an attempted suicide, and finally a divorce and a life as a single mom, with all its challenges. I just wanted to scream at the doctor who did the procedure and let him know that it was not over in thirty minutes. This nightmare affected me for a lifetime.

Four years later, hope was on the horizon. God's plan for me led me to my present husband of thirty years. With him, I have survived many crossroads filled with rebellious children, sickness, the death of loved ones, and loss of jobs – yet he loved me unconditionally. He could not understand my deep-seeded feelings of shame and guilt from a mistake I had made in the past. I had kept this secret for over thirty years. I was parched and thirsty for relief, looking for a well in this desert of pain.

Then out of desperation, I turned to Jesus for help and hope, but my hurt was so deep that it took another seven years, going through many disappointments, and most importantly not being able to let go of past mistakes. Life has a way of presenting you with a horrible tragedy that is wrapped up in a beautiful gift box waiting for you to peel off the paper and find inner strength. I was diagnosed with breast cancer. Yes, the ultimate crossroad. My life came to a screeching halt.

Now I turn my attention to the women and men reading this story. The above is an event in my life that might have happened to you also. As you can now see, the last crossroad for me was when I came to the end of myself and had no choice but surrender. This was when I met my Savior face to face and heard his sweet voice whisper in my ears of how much He loved me and that "I WAS WHOLE AND HEALED BY HIS STRIPES." This happened at Mount Sinai Hospital on December 13, 2010, just when I had been told that I had a 16% chance to live.

I was overwhelmed, but at the same time filled with instant peace.

His peace.

For some of you right now you are skeptical and do not believe in miracles. That is okay because He loves you so much and has so much grace as well as mercy that He will allow you to make the decision to reveal Himself to you. I spent the next six months developing my relationship with Him and was freed of all bitterness, anger, and forgave all who hurt me. I had no more jealousy and apologized to my husband and my children for the hurts that I may have caused in their lives. My broken and shattered heart was touched by a father's love from above, and in return gave me a life free of shame and guilt for the horrible mistake I made in having an abortion.

This is when my crossroad to true healing happened. I was now truly a whole person and could live my life with true joy and peace.

I meditated on many verses to help me overcome my feeling of guilt and shame. Trust me, you need to know that you too are worthy of total forgiveness and find inner healing by forgiving yourselves as well.

He created you in your mother's womb, He has great plans for you, and nothing you do is a surprise to Him. If you look up the word laminin, it is the glue that holds your cells together in your DNA. Inside there is a shape of a cross – His imprint is in your DNA.

He knows the number of hairs you have on your head. Don't be afraid; He takes care of the birds and the flowers in the fields, therefore to Him you are definitely more valued and loved than them. He knows every aspect of your body, mind, soul as well as all your needs. Can you imagine that!

The Lord has great plans for you. He wants to aid you and not harm you; He wants to give you hope and a future. He will guide you through your challenges, disappointments, failures, and hardships of life because His promises are true and you can count on them. God loved you so much that gave his one and only Son, Jesus, to die for you. The power of his death on the cross is all about this statement, "It is finished." That statement was just for you, He has forgiven you for every mistake and wrong you have done in the past, present and in the future. You are now in right-standing with God. No more guilt, shame, bitterness, anger, revenge or jealousy. You will be filled with His love because He took all your hurts to the Cross. He has forgiven you! For the men reading this, I plead with you to get involved, be supportive and please do not judge her decision. Remember it is your love and compassion that will heal her heart.

You too will also have joy once again and will live a vibrant life that looks like a rainbow after a thunderstorm. Today I have total health. I now have a degree in nursing, and practice as a health educator and diet counselor. I teach people the benefits of disease prevention, which includes inner healing as well as outer healing and impacting people's lives every day. I have childlike faith despite the event in my life that could have stolen every joy that God had planned for me.

I now live my life with gratitude every day, because of the blessings He has given me in life. There are too many for me to mention, but I will share just this one. I now have a new son, I call him my adoptive son, and his name is Charlie. He came into my life with his wife Adrianna at the same time that I discovered I had cancer. He was there for every step climbing the mountain in my fight against cancer.

The miracle is in God's timing because the child that I aborted would have been born at the same time that Charlie was born. Yes, God does heal all wounds and meets you at every crossroad in your life. Just receive it and believe it. God is in the details. God is in the moment. God is in all parts of your life, even the hurts in life.

Life is like a dessert. Too brief to hurry. On the other hand, too short not to let Him in your life.

What is healing? We all have a different perspective of this powerful word. As for me, it is knowing that Christ lives in me and nothing is impossible because He loves me. I will leave you with a parting message that children are like angels from heaven and working with them as a nurse gave me back my childlike faith once more. Because when you look in their eyes, that is what you see. They want to get better and they just believe. You too can be healed. Just believe!

This is a special message to women contemplating an abortion; there is a heartbeat at day twenty-one, brainwaves on day forty-five! That's right, even before you know there is a pregnancy. This is a special gift from God and He will bring you through this with His love and promises.

You too can be a whole person and have your crossroad to healing.

Let your heart be healed. Just let Him in, He will be the greatest connection and relationship you will ever have for living your life without limitations.

Born in Montreal, Gloria Callan acquired the knowledge of many languages while living a vibrant life. Her educational background includes an RN degree (with over twenty years' experience) and marketing degree in the fashion industry, which makes her very flexible to an individual's needs. Her research and extensive travels in Europe and South America led her to a degree as a Health Educator and Diet Counselor. Gloria faced and survived cancer herself without conventional medicine. She now teaches clients to take control of their health through the process of nutrition and lifestyle changes to reverse the effects of many acute and chronic diseases.

Email: **bglo@rogers.com**

Compiled by Anita Sechesky

CHAPTER TWENTY-SIX

Break Through the Bullying
by Nathaniel Sechesky

My first experience with bullying happened when I was in Grade One. It was a gloomy and rainy day, and some of my classmates wanted the new baseball hat that I had received as a gift from my grandparents. The boys grabbed it from me and when I chased them to get it back, they began throwing it around in the air. Then one of the boys who had my hat threw it into a large mud puddle and stepped on it, splashing me as well. I wasn't happy at all about this, but I tried to avoid telling my parents about what happened because I was confused, and I didn't understand why the boys, who were like my best friends the day before, changed the way they were acting towards me that day. I was upset because it was my newest hat and when I got the attention of the schoolyard supervisor and asked her for help, she looked annoyingly at me and said, "Well, what do you want me to do about it?" She was busy on her cell phone. Now that I think about it, she was not one of our teachers, but only a volunteer who obviously was not trained to look out for students' well-being while on schoolyard duty.

Looking back, this is definitely an area that concerns me greatly because many schools bring in volunteers that go through their basic backgrounds checks who are then very enthusiastic that they're part of the educational system making a difference in young people's lives, but do they really understand the impact they will make if they don't intervene when most needed? I'm very sure, based on the rise of bullying that happens in the younger grades, that many of these volunteers are still holding back from getting actively involved to stop bullying in its tracks. Only time will tell.

When my mom picked me up at school, she noticed that my new

hat was dirty and wet and asked me what I did to it. I had no choice but to tell her about the bullies in my class. If you know my mom, she is a very determined person and did not let this go. When we got home, she was on the phone with the school and told the principal her and my dad were coming in to speak with them. After an unusually long wait time at the school office, my parents finally got an opportunity to speak with the principal regarding their concerns about the incident. They were told that basically the school was not taking the blame for the recess supervisor who claimed she did not see anything even though I saw her turn around and look my way when she heard what was happening. The next day, my mom walked me to my classroom to speak with my teacher who was already informed of this incident and had just spoken to the other boys. When they saw me, they apologized to me. This experience might seem minor compared to what I have heard some of my friends have gone through, and it's one of the reasons why I decided to write *"The BullyCode - Broken People Create More Broken People."*

Based on my experience and what my friends have gone through, I believe bullies are a product of their environment, and when someone is treated a certain way, that is how they will treat others. The victims of bullies are people who end up having low self-esteem and live in fear of what others are thinking about them constantly.

We can all make a difference in the way we treat others because we don't know what others are going through in their lives. People who look to destroy others have no confidence to do better.

The world is a pretty tough place, and if you want to become somebody in this world, you have to have a strong mind not to allow anyone to break your spirit. It's hard enough trying to fit in as a young person when people are so quick to judge and make fun of others. Maybe your parents or family members were bullied, and you don't have a lot of positive influences in your life. You don't have to go through what they did. There's lots of resources on Social Media to motivate and encourage you to become the best you can be. Our world needs to teach more acceptance of all people regardless of who they are. Everyone has feelings and deserves a fair chance to become all they can be without the frustrations, fears, hurts, and destructive attitudes of others projected on them. Sadly, there are too many people who don't know what to do when they are bullied, they don't know how to help themselves, and what ends up happening is they are at risk of hurting themselves because of this. I believe that bystanders can do a lot more than sitting back and watch others being victimized. I hope that our generation will start to care more for each other, instead of pretending they are blind and looking the other way.

You don't have to be broken and damaged anymore. There's really no excuse once you have access to the internet or read books like this that help you to believe in yourself first so that you can help others. People who look to destroy others have no confidence to do better and are lacking the wisdom to understand that it's not healthy to project their behaviors and attitudes. These same kinds of people are usually the ones who will need the most help when they grow up because they will be expected to behave certain ways as productive members of society. Bullies will only grow up to be adult bullies, and victims of bullies will grow up to people who are still damaged if they are not connected to a positive outlet of support.

Steps to Stop a Bully:

1. Recognize the wrong and write it down – document everything that you see a bully doing to others or yourself. What's the Date? Where did this happen? Can you describe the place? What are the names of witnesses or bystanders? What time did all this happen? What was everyone wearing? What may have caused the incident to happen in the first place?

2. Try to figure out what is going on with the Bully – is this a regular occurrence that they pick on someone new or different? Who else have they done this to? What was the outcome of past incidents? How often have you or anyone else witnessed or been aware of these behaviors?

3. Speak to any and all bystanders – find out why they didn't stop the bully. Did they feel threatened? Is there any way they could have stopped it? Did they have a cellphone to call a teacher, adult or authorities or record the incident? Everyone is quick to record it, but did they report it?

4. Report the bully – submit as much documentation on the incident to those in charge, either at school, a bus driver, school security, your parents, a place of employment, a police department and make sure it is reported to more than one adult.

Since I was born in 2001, my Generation Z has a lot of work to do to help stop bullying as it has become worse year after year, more than it's ever been before. You have to wonder if people have a sick fascination with watching others get hurt. If this is the case, then we need to be more proactive and stop bullying before it even starts – with education on equality and acceptance for all. Abuse in any form should never be tolerated in this day and age. You just have to go on Social Media and see what the effects of bullying has done to so many lives and sadly, too many victims, who have been neglected or silent in their abuse, have ended up in detrimental circumstances. It's time for everyone to open their eyes and realize that with the rise of mental health awareness in our society, too many people are suffering needlessly right under our noses.

Strong people don't hurt others weaker than themselves.

Nathaniel Sechesky is a senior high school student who has successfully completed his first certification in Computer Programming and is actively completing his second certification of C++ programming. He enjoys working on his YouTube channel, Multimedia arts, playing video games, Tae Kwon Do, and playing squash. Nathaniel is the visionary and co-author of the book *The BullyCode - Broken People Create More Broken People* for all age groups which will be published Spring 2018.

Youtube: **https://bit.ly/2qqsRRu**

Compiled by Anita Sechesky

CHAPTER TWENTY-SEVEN

A Stumble along the Crooked Path: A Chapter from My "Book of Life"

by Satie Narain-Simon

Wedding Day! I pinched myself, exuding in the syrup of happiness. Finally "getting off the shelf" as so many would say. After all, there were so many single years. It was quite a bumpy road on the "Avenue of Love."

> *Today I get to watch my parents' faces as they get ready for the event. I noticed their peace and contentment. My father couldn't be prouder. It made my heart smile. It was over a decade ago where a wedding was taking place – mine. It did not happen to cause unsurmountable grief and pain. Today, I feel the quiet happiness within me and my parents. Everything is falling into place so easily: the Italian hall all decked out with pink, yellow, and white; the lawn where the ceremony would take place; food and entertainment all just so easy putting together. It is almost as if the heavens are celebrating too. Such a glorious sunny day, loving the feel of my wedding dress with its latticework so beautifully done, wondering how my Californian love is doing. It's his family's first trip to Toronto as they traveled from California, Las Vegas, and Idaho to be here. Thoughts shift to my upcoming move to California, leaving behind my family here. Love it there in California: the mountains, the weather, the ocean, wine country – we have so many plans for the future.*

That was over thirteen years ago!

It was one week prior to the big day, exuberant indeed. Excitedly gabbing with my New York girlfriend about her flight plans when suddenly my hand moved across my chest...a lump! I jumped out of bed and scaled across the hall to the washroom, raised my arms, and there it was – a lump hard as ever in the six o'clock position under my left breast!

My world turned upside down in an instant! This couldn't be happening. The doctors made a mistake we all thought. What happened? I was this "happy go lucky" individual with a personal belief of living each day as charitably as possible: a smile to strangers, giving a compliment to a female, volunteering at the Intensive Care Unit, preparing for my black belt in Tae Kwon-Do, eating healthy, drinking my vitamins! I am bulletproof for a long healthy life!

Not realizing that creeping into my subconscious was the years spent in a quicksand of dark thoughts feeding into my cells. Something was brewing!

I was diagnosed with breast cancer at the happiest time of my life. I spent years in the school called "Mind" training, reprogramming my mind to thought awareness, slowly climbing out the "black hole" of darkness. I had spent years in emotional crisis – life's struggles, of course, the biggest one, affairs of the heart. Struggles of lack – lack of self-esteem, lack of confidence, lack of self-love, lack, lack, lack…I am in a place of my finding myself, my authentic self. I had learned to love myself exactly the way I am, with all the little imperfections. My imperfections became perfect because I love myself. I am worthy, I am beautiful, I believe in ME! I do not depend on someone else to validate me. When I look back, it was all those of dark cryptic thoughts breaking down the shields of auric fields penetrating on a cellular level. I do believe cells remember trauma because they have an intelligence. I paid the price for weak emotions! I do believe in Darwin's theory "Survival of the Fittest!" All those years, the cells were crying and losing hope. They just couldn't take it anymore and "Boom!" became cancerous!

Day of Surgery

I had my CD player with my healing mantra – my spiritual grandfather, Swami Veda Bharati of the Himalayan Tradition, told me to do so. There we were, my family and I, in agony! I felt fear and trying so hard to hold on to hope. I knew in my heart something was not right. My husband and I huddled, clutching to my pics of Saints dear friends gave me: Patron St. Peregrine (Patron Saint for Cancer) and Lord Khrishna…my thoughts racing to the Supreme. A nurse came by saying, "Not to worry, the lump is a fibroid." My husband and I looked at each other with such relief.

We will have a glass of wine and watch our wedding video. Just as the thought was about to complete, the surgeon appeared looking grim and straight ahead. All I heard was, "Cancer, don't know where it spread...mastectomy..." His voice faded, everyone staring! I was not there anymore. My body was but my mind drifted. No one could help me. I called out to God, my Father for help. Suddenly this nurse showed up standing in front of me. I recognized the accent; it was the familiar sunshine Caribbean tone. She started praying and said with authority in her voice, "With conviction, you are saved." She disappeared and then two young doctors showed up, each taking a hand. I could sense their sadness. I felt like a child and the Lord was guiding their actions. The nurse appeared again and looked straight into my eyes as they prepared me for surgery. She was praying in a very loud authoritative voice. I was staring into her pupils as everything went black.

I suddenly felt/sensed this soft beautiful white light glowing over me. I was smiling and excited. I was giggling, communicating with something and felt so happy. My hand glided over to my left side and thought "Oh, I have my breast" and then my awareness was back to this reality. By the way, I tried searching for THAT nurse, but no one has heard or ever seen her. I truly believe she was an angel!

Chemo!

The cancer growth was aggressive, HER2 triple-negative. My body was young and the cancer took charge. Chemo broke me – it broke my mind, body, and spirit. I remember distinctly one incident when I was trying to concentrate on the Supreme Father and I just couldn't. I felt like a zombie. I had no thoughts; it was so weird. I had to rebuild from each level. Each cell was crying. It was tough, sad, and scary so many times. The psychological pain was difficult, looking into to the mirror and not recognizing the person staring back. Losing my hair, I felt anger. I loved my hair! I was torn. I knew I would lose my hair, I was prepared but when the time came, I was not prepared! In a sweep of three times, all my hair was gone. One night I went to brush my teeth and I couldn't – my gums bled because the brush was too tough, so I had to use my fingers. I couldn't taste – everything tasted like metal. My stomach felt upset most days and the list went on. My body, my organs, my cells were crying! But it was also at that time, I had an opportunity to grow. Time to strengthen my bond with the Higher Power!

I kept positive and couldn't have done it without my family's support. My husband loved me exactly the way I was. They were all amazing, my Heroes, my iron shield! My brother was like a soldier – no one was allowed to entertain any negativity. During chemo sessions, my entire family accompanied me, including my husband making his way from California. I was fed with nutrients every two hours if and when my stomach was in agreement. I never for one moment considered dying. I felt it was just a "major bump" along my crooked path! Soon all will be well – a new day is coming. The key to my success was never, ever considering a negative thought!

A New Day!

At the time of diagnosis, I was not aware my brother was conducting a worldwide research for alternative help. He was convinced that there was more than just Western medicine for me. There I was at the start of an amazing "out of this world" journey! At first, I was skeptical. Could it be true...Miracles? Logic and illogical minds were in conflict. Secretly, I was hoping and very excited!

Three weeks after my last radiation treatment, I was on a plane with my brother to an unknown remote little area, called Abadiania, located off central Brazil to a well-researched documented phenomenon taking place. There is a man known as the Miracle Man of Brazil...no logical explanation. He is probably the most powerful medium alive and must rank amongst the greatest physic surgeons of this 21st century. His "gift" is not hereditary or learned from books. His body being used as an instrument for Spiritual Entities to incorporate, giving himself over to healing and serving others. Trust me, it was mind boggling until I became a witness.

As the car pulled onto the unassuming red brick road, I began to feel different – nervous, shaky, and excited to the core in anticipation. I remember the first time walking to the center, I sensed a peaceful, sacred quietness! There was a "stillness" that speaking sounded like noise to my ear. This area has a very high energy field and is built on land rich in natural quartz, which is also a powerful energy source. This place was magical! I can't seem to find the words to express what one feels here, your thoughts, emotions... it's like "worry" does not exist. There is a definite "Presence" and its feeling of unconditional love cannot be overshadowed.

Most of the healings performed by the Medium are invisible, or instantaneous. Demonstrations of physical surgery, "visible operations," are specifically performed to enable people to "see" the

Entities at work. This is done to fulfill the Center's mission of not only healing the sick but also of providing irrefutable proof that there is another dimension – a Spirit world, where we all eventually will go when this physical life expires!

Imagine witnessing a physical surgery with only a few drops of blood or no anesthetic? How is this possible? I have witnessed this numerous times – my very first time I was with my brother. We just stood there, a foot away, almost in a trance, looking at this beautiful young American girl having a physical surgery and not even flinching. She looked so calm and serene – less than ten drops of blood fell on her white pants. We were so overwhelmed emotionally that words cannot express! Our definition of "normal" was redefined.

Something happened in Abadiania! My mind, body, and soul were affected by a source of unconditional love. My Spirit was excited, dancing and overjoyed! I understood as to why I got sick in the first place – I reconnected and strengthened my bond to the higher Source! I felt like a child, innocent and happy. I know I am being taken care of, I know I am truly loved and really have nothing to worry about.

I had the opportunity to forgive myself for the contribution to the disease – dark, cryptic thoughts and the guilt I felt for wasting so many precious youthful years on weak emotions. I felt the Entities working on me. I am of absolute surety that I was diagnosed for a reason. I feel a fire burning in my soul and it's all about serving others – this is the ultimate of my true authentic Self. This is where I am supposed to be, on my "Perfect Crooked Path!"

My life began. My Truth, my Essence! Father nudging his Child! "I AM" the answer to my thoughts!

With love, Satie

Satie Narain-Simon, originally from Guyana (SA), resides in Toronto. She is a Chartered Professional Accountant, works as a Tax Auditor with the Canadian Federal Government, is an avid traveler, a member of Toastmasters, practices Reiki, has a Black Stripe belt in Tae-Kwon Do, and is an initiate of Swami Veda Bharati - lineage of the Himalayan tradition of yoga and meditation. Satie cherishes her spiritual journeys to Brazil and prides herself as a Guide to her spiritual home. She was honored as a "Daughter of the Casa Dom Inacio" by the "Entities of Light" in 2012 and is an International speaker – award recipient of (WEF) Woman Economic Forum.

LinkedIn: **https://www.linkedin.com/satienarainsimon/**

Website: **https://www.Casasdehealing.com**

Compiled by Anita Sechesky

WORDS OF ENCOURAGEMENT

No matter where you end up, never forget where you started! Always remember: no matter how bad a situation you are in — or think you are in — there is someone out in the world who has it 100% worse! Keep Pushin' Forward Always!

SUJIT K. REDDY

Compiled by Anita Sechesky

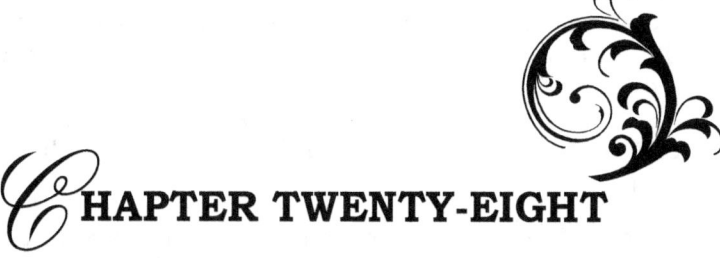

CHAPTER TWENTY-EIGHT

Healing My Spirit and Broken Wing
by Elizabeth Ann Pennington

I FORGIVE. Those two words are the most important and precious words in life, at least in mine.

I have three sisters, five brothers, my mommy, daddy and a grandmother we all call "Mother." We live on a farm in a very small community called Lily, Kentucky. We grow our own vegetables in the summer, canning them as they are ready and enjoying them in the winter. We also raise hogs and cattle and preserve our own meat. My clothes are homemade; I'm the grandest and best dressed little girl in the neighborhood. I love the winter time because I get two new nightgowns made of "outing" material and they match my mommy's gowns. I'm blessed, most of all blessed with lots of love and attention, being the last born and very much unexpected. That's another story!

When I think back to my childhood to tell my story, I really don't know where to start; my life has been very complicated. Here is how life looked to me in childhood:

My daddy has died and it's my fault...

My brother, just older than myself, and I are in grade school; I am only seven. Another brother is in college. The rest of my brothers and sisters have married. Daddy is postmaster at Lily, and Mommy helps him in the office. The Post Office is next door to our home, so every day after school I go straight to see Daddy to give him a hug and kiss.

Today, Mother gets my brother and me ready for school; Mommy and Daddy have already gone to work. After school, I am so excited about a girlfriend coming to play with me I go home to change into play clothes instead of going to see Daddy. While I am changing clothes, my brother comes running into the house screaming "Daddy's dead." I was Daddy's girl, and my world just stopped. It could not be true. I ran to the Post Office only to be stopped from entering. I thought that he had died because I didn't give him a hug and kiss!

I still have Mommy, Mother, and brother at home, but it is not the same; I'm helpless. I once saw a bird with a broken wing; that is how I feel, broken.

As time passes, Mommy makes my brother let me go with him to do chores. This means just let me go along, I think! He takes me with him but I know he doesn't like taking his little sister with him when milking the cows, feeding the pigs and chickens. I think it's fun, but my brother doesn't. I'm having so much fun, just being with my brother, "helping" him.

This brother was not the only one I seemed to bother with my tagalongs. Once when my brother that was in college came home, Mommy insisted he and his girlfriend (now his wife) take me bowling with them. I don't think the girlfriend liked my tagging along; they didn't talk the whole way home. Mommy said it was because I beat the girlfriend's score! I'm not so sure and don't know what I have done wrong this time.

No matter the occasion, whether it is at school, at church or a community activity, I had to attend. Supposedly, keeping me busy will help me get over Daddy's death and feeling lonely.

I am now a teenager, and either too young or too old. "You cannot do that you are a girl." "You're too young," or "You cannot do that; you are too old." Please! Where do I fit in?

Skipping a few years...

I want to tell someone but can't tell anyone what's happen. Someone very close to me, someone I love and look up to has betrayed me. I'm only fourteen. I'm being sexually molested. I don't know what to do. Do I dare tell? He will be mad and not love me anymore; my sister will not believe me and will stop loving me. I've tried to stop him from touching me, but he tells me I'm going to be the one in trouble – it's my fault. People will think I'm bad, no good. I must not tell anyone, just keep it a secret here in my hiding place and hope it stops. I just have to make sure there's no possible way he will be alone with me. My spirit has been stolen.

It had started with just a touch at first; one made by accident I thought. Then it happened again and again. I tried stopping him by raising my voice telling him to stop. When someone would check to see what was happening he made a joke of it saying, "Oh, we were just horsing around."

Then he started asking Mommy's permission to let me go places with him. He always asks her in a way that indicated I wanted to go. Sometimes I could talk my way out of going. Unfortunately, there were too many times I failed.

The touching escalated. He started running his hands to places they had no business going. Then, the day came that forever altered my life.

As time passes me by...

I continue to feel guilt for my daddy's death. I pray the time will come that I will understand.

It is difficult to describe my feelings of the molestation. Emotions of fear, hurt, and guilt would be only a start. The feeling of abandonment is like a shadow holding me hostage. Trusting is very tough.

Countless times I've wanted to speak out, only to doubt myself. Would it be the best thing to do, will it open doors of criticism and shame to my family? What will my family and friends think of me? Will friends continue to call me friend? Will family support me?

Until the right time, I must hide my tears behind a smile and my fears behind a positive attitude.

In reflection of my past, I suffered quietly for many years after Daddy died. I was just a little girl who lost her father; it happens, right? My family tried to fill my life with what they thought was best for me, and I will always love them for that. However, what I needed was to understand Daddy's death. What I heard that day was Daddy's heart broke. To me, I broke it and I would have rather have died than to have broken Daddy's heart.

Years later, while talking with my brother, I spoke of my feelings. To my surprise, he told me he had blamed himself for Daddy's death. This opened my eyes; no one knows what's in someone else's mind, how they perceive life, and how a little thing like a word can change your life forever. After the conversation with my brother, my broken wing started to heal. I no longer felt alone. Someone else has felt the same as me.

Until you let go of what you are holding in, you will never heal. I encourage everyone; please speak with someone, a family member, a friend or a professional.

Fitting in is not important to anyone except oneself. The only place anyone should worry about fitting in is with themselves and what they believe in. Nothing or no one else matters as much. I can say from personal experience of trying to "fit in," one will only find heartache and hurt feelings, not to mention the loss of time and energy so critical to having a wonderful life. With help, I took inventory of my life to separate what I needed to hang onto and what to let go of.

Violation of one's person is something that takes time to heal. I will forever have the memory but I no longer will let it hurt me. I kept this secret for most of my life until one night a deep voice from inside said to me, "It's time to let go." Even though scared, I did. Time stood still with flashbacks of those horrible times rolling in fast as I spoke. However, after the words, "I've been molested" left my lips, I could feel my spirit freed.

Healing starts first by forgiving oneself; I accepted I had done nothing wrong. If something similar has happened to you, chances are you have done nothing either. You are the same wonderful person; being molested doesn't mean you're evil or bad.

After forgiving yourself, forgiving the person that molested you is a crucial final step. It has taken a lot of prayers and tears to get me to this place in life. I'm no longer afraid to look in the mirror.

Sharing my secret with the world gives strength to my healing. Ultimate healing will come when someone else's spirit and broken wing begins to heal after reading this chapter of my life.

Forgive yourself and others. Christ Jesus has and will forgive us

Compiled by Anita Sechesky

Elizabeth Ann Pennington became a Best-Selling International Author in 2013 and since has participated in multiple best-selling books. As an author, she shares encouragement and confidence to live your life to the fullest, not letting disappointments or fear stand in your way. Elizabeth is a certified Life Enhancement Coach, Speaker, Trainer, and Mentor. She also offers PTSD and other trauma clients, both individual and family, guidance toward a refreshing balance in quality of life. Elizabeth worked in both the corporate and private world for forty plus years, and now enjoys working from home as an Author, Coach and Internet Marketer.

Facebook: **facebook.com/The-Age-to-Learn-Building-Confidence-One...**

LinkedIn: **linkedin.com/in/elizabeth-pennington- 85b73587**

More Stories to Heal Your World Now

Compiled by Anita Sechesky

CHAPTER TWENTY-NINE

I Was Living on the Edge
by Stacey Cargnelutti

"Mom, what's your biggest regret?" asked my twelve-year-old son. "Hmmm, I don't have any regrets...just lessons learned," I cautiously responded. "Mom, what's the worst thing you ever did?" "Ugh!" I thought, "I'm not getting off the hook here am I?"

After a sobering moment, I humbly replied, "The lies."

~~~~~~~~

There was something about living on "the edge" that made me feel alive... and something about hiding that made me feel safe.

On the outside I appeared quiet, but on the inside, the noise resounded continually. Soon I found ways to escape it and began to live a double life as a result.

I listened hard, to anyone, and I watched...a lot. I was sincerely intrigued with people. But in all my observations, I neglected to develop my own identity, discover my own values, and connect with my own source of inspiration.

By the age of twelve, I had already put on a mask of deceit and come to some serious resolutions on how I would live life. As I continued in conversation with my son, it seemed that he was also coming to some resolutions of his own, at the ripe old age of twelve.

~~~~~~~~

It was an astounding experience to look at college photos and wonder, "Who is that?" As I turned the pages, attempting to reminisce, I couldn't find the person in the photos, she was empty, void of substance, yet full of such presence.

Although I knew the strength of my will and the longing of my heart, I couldn't seem to connect as I continued through the album. I carried a deep desire to know love, just as every human soul, but hadn't found my worth or met my Maker.

I saw fear, along with a desperate need to know and be known, but I would lose myself in a relationship, making the prospect of intimacy terrifying.

The pervasive darkness in my green eyes spoke not only of an absence of light, but sadness, shame, and heaviness. Although comfortable teaching and performing, I hid behind alcohol and other vices to mask insecurity.

I learned to carry the emotional needs of others through cautious behavior. I chose "what, how and when," according to "their vibes" rather than my own. Ultimately, I gave my power away by allowing fear-based anger to control me.

I was the queen of deceit, well able to put on a happy face while submerged in a sea of defiance and passive aggression; soon I would be washed ashore.

By the age of twenty-three, my goals were met and I thought I'd let loose and enjoy life a bit. Short of having kids and becoming a published author, I thought I had "arrived." HA!

New career, marriage, condo, mortgage, dog, friends, car... Now what? Within months, my lack of vision resulted in complete lawlessness, and this "disciplined doer" suddenly cast off all restraint and began to live her already "double life" with greater fervency than ever before. The defiant chameleon learned how to put on many fronts.

Years of lying, stealing, addiction, compulsion, eating disorders, selfish ambition, two abortions, two adulterous relationships, a totaled car, arrest for drunk driving, and a few hours in jail with a cell full of prostitutes, resulted.

My deep-seated belief that "love is dangerous," continued to confirm itself as I sabotaged every attempt at true connection and intimacy. Before long, I found myself in a deceptive web that, although begun in childhood, was now ready to trap and choke out whatever life and hope were left in me.

Interestingly, in the midst of the dark mess I had created, I continued to play at the top of my "game," working hard, eating little, and sharing my passion for health and fitness all at the same time. Working in the fitness industry fueled my dysfunction beautifully.

I taught eight fitness classes to kids every day then headed off to meet my cardio junkies at the gym for some high flying, old-school aerobics that left me drenched and depleted. Sitting down in the shower for fear of fainting became the norm, then onto graduate school before retiring.

I ate just enough to fuel my exercise addiction and enough to keep from being labeled "anorexic." My husband worked nights, which gave me plenty of time to enjoy the "pleasures of adultery" and abuse my body to star in workout videos on the side.

Awarded "Teacher of the Year!" And within twenty-four hours of receiving the prize money, I rented an apartment and left my husband. In the midst of my silent rage, he continued to ask, "When are we going to have kids?"

"How could you dare bring kids into this lie?!" "How can you pretend things are good, brag about me, and not even know me???" I was convinced these questions justified my defiance.

I never learned to identify my emotions, much less articulate them in order to be known and relieve the pain of feeling invisible. So like many, I found some things to keep me numb.

Desperately seeking answers and waaay past due for some enlightenment, I began the deep work of self-discovery and soon realized the edge I was living on would lead me to glory if I stayed the course and got courageously honest about some things.

I became a tenacious truth seeker, and at the age of thirty, life as I knew it came to a screeching halt, and all things became new.

Continual contemplation, journaling, meditation, prayer, and Bible study became my new way. A different twelve-step meeting each night, along with writing assignments from my therapist, kept me in a continual state of awareness and intense mindfulness.

Letting go of illusion and fear was difficult. Discovering the faulty belief system driving my life was painful. But my determination to dispel darkness and live under an open heaven was supernatural.

All the emotion I had buried in those silent years began to move through me and break the chains of self-imposed captivity I had always known. It was uncomfortable, but if the truth were to set me free, deceit had to flee.

I could feel the sadness of letting go, along with the joy of a new and safe embrace. I rejoiced in the responsibility of choice. My newfound ability to reject fear and choose love inspired and empowered me.

I Share my Story...

...in the hope of setting you free from the cunning ways of deception. I pray that you might know a life without limitations and live in the love from which you came.

The freedom I've come to know is nothing more than the result of getting honest and renewing my mind to the truth of God's word. Darkness needed to flee, and all emotional ties to the lies had to be severed. In order to live differently, I, as well as you, must think, feel and act differently.

The most empowering truth I want to leave you with is that your heart holds the beliefs framing your life. They determine your thoughts, words, and ways. And until your heart breaks up with fear and unites with love, you will continue to sabotage the deep and true riches of life and intimacy you are designed and destined for.

You hold the thoughts, feelings, and intentions of God's heart but

choosing to align with them requires serious intention. Divine life and lasting change come only through the working out of the Christ mind within you through hearing and reading and meditating and applying.

Please know that when you choose to live from a divine and infinite mind, deceit and darkness won't stand a chance.

To experience real life and lasting change, a letting go of the sensual in exchange for the spiritual must occur. You may need to leave relationships, and the patterns and systems of behavior that no longer serve the divine in you and embracing the ones that do.

Seeing things from heaven's perspective enables you to make sense out of your experiences and find purpose in and through your pain. As you consume a daily dose of spirit and truth, your thoughts will align with heaven, and your words will usher in the abundant life you're here to know.

The voices of defeat, lack and limitation can be overwhelming, but those voices hold only the power you give them. Know that in this one practice of putting off lies and putting on truth, you can expect to see the goodness of God here and now.

Nothing is impossible to the one who believes.

Close your eyes, and see with your spiritual eyes, hear with your spiritual ears, and find the real, true, authentic you. Now let that one arise!

Your start was not about you, but your finish is, and you get to write it! Until your story ends in glory, you're not done.

The gift of redemption is the absolute goodness and grace bestowed upon all those willing to go deep and discover the hindrances that keep them bound to a shallow and sensual life.

You, dear friend, are equipped and empowered to be all and do all. You've got what it takes to overcome and conquer the inevitable obstacles along your way. Make no bones about it; you are graced for your race!

Let your ashes be turned to beauty and your mourning to dancing as you pursue, conquer and recover all that's been stolen and know complete restoration of all.

Here's to your greatest triumph, deepest love and brightest tomorrows.

Much love,

Stacey Cargnelutti

Stacey Cargnelutti's work as an author, speaker and coach is thought-provoking and life-changing! Her latest book titled Egypt 2 Canaan - A Guide to Lasting Change & Rich Fulfillment is supported by her High Powered Success Academy and VIP UPLevel coaching programs. Stacey has a candid way of confronting complacency and empowering you to live an inspired life of freedom and abundance. Her love for people and positive energy are nothing less than contagious and her promise to you is truth over tactics.

Email: **Stacey@StaceyC.com**

Facebook: **StaceyC**

Compiled by Anita Sechesky

CHAPTER THIRTY

I Was That Little Girl
by Carol Metz Murray

Imagine yourself as a child, filled with love, laughter, and life. The world is your oyster; beauty surrounds you; love and safety are held near and dear without knowing or naming them. As that child, you skipped carefree through a meadow totally mesmerized by the sights, sounds, smells. Life is good. Curiosity abounds. Then blackness begins to color the rainbow of curiosity. Laughter silently slips away locked in a time warp. Love feels hollow and life loses its luster. A cloak of painful secrecy veils you, your voice becomes a whisper; and no one comes to help. I remember the debilitating pain, the silence, the humiliation, the aloneness, the fear, the anger and feeling so overwhelmingly unsafe.

I recall asking many questions that remained unanswered:

- Doesn't anyone care about what has just happened to me?
- Why am I all alone in this darkness and silence?
- What must I do to be accepted and loved?
- Mommy, why am I a "bad" girl; what does it mean that "good girls don't do that?"

This is my story. When I was a little girl I was known as Suzie. At the age of six, I was sexually molested by a neighbor.

What had been a normal, openhearted childhood, turned into a world of fear, confusion, shame, guilt, and silence! I tried so hard to talk to my mother, but she couldn't or wouldn't hear me. My young voice was dismissed. I tried so hard to understand what this was all about. What had I done to make this happen to me?

The only one who acknowledged my fear was my Alsatian dog, Rocky. He would growl at this attacker or guard me, keeping him at bay. He was my protector, but unfortunately, Rocky was not always at my side.

I was on my own, living in a trapped world of terror and silence with no one to turn too. Fear and anxiety filled my soul. There was only me to protect me and keep me safe. I dared not get angry, dared not to scream out, good girls didn't do that. I felt so alone and so scared.

The molestations continued for many years. Confusion and guilt filled me. My heart slapped shut. When I was twelve, they stopped. But still, no one would acknowledge these abominable experiences, much less ask me what lay at the hidden base of the fear, anxiety, stress and emotional void.

When I was nineteen, I was raped. "There must be something wrong with me," so, as an adult, I entered relationships based on what I knew: Silence, Abuse, and no Self-Worth.

By the age of twenty-five, I had four beautiful babies; and a violence-filled marriage. I knew that if I stayed – I would surely die. Despite my lack of self-worth, and having no one to turn to, I made the move – alone. Step-by-step I began to rebuild my life – along the way unearthing my courage, finding my spirit, and, once again, opening my heart. The strength that I found to leave my marriage helped me raise my children, get work and rise through the ranks until I sustained a respected career and earned my Master's degree.

But the pain filled history of Susie's past wouldn't go away. Just after I turned forty, I hit the wall. It was time to ask for help. But could I or would I ask for help? Who could I trust? I felt like a deflated being. My Soul burst with a tsunami of tears that continued to flood my life day after day, releasing one trapped emotion after another. Through the dense fog, I attempted to analyze what had happened, not yet recognizing that after years of abuse my self-worth had been beaten to a pulp. My self-respect was nonexistent. Self-love wasn't even in my vocabulary or on my radar. My health was in tatters. I didn't understand the fierce anger exploding within me like an endless inferno. My dream career had gone up in smoke. How was I to keep my dignity? I felt frustrated that others did not understand. I suffered many losses as my world imploded. I wallowed in fear and anxiety for days on end, attempting to remember my name. I wondered, "Who am I?"

During these depressing times, the pain was excruciating and relentless. I felt exposed and isolated, yet denial reigned supreme. Who would listen to me now; no one had before. Past support had been very limited and I had long ago been discouraged by the victim-blaming reactions of others. Their questions suggested they thought there was something "wrong" with me. Who now would really believe that I, who appeared so together on the outside, was tattered and torn and void on the inside? The torture, the fight, the struggle, how could I believe myself or admit that there was really, really anything wrong with me or my life?

I remember I would hold my head high and say to myself "stand tall, be tall." I had been the independent, self-reliant, strong-willed little girl turned woman who knew how to take care of herself. Trapped inside my blocked emotions, shame consumed me; guilt ate me up; anger poured out of every orifice of my being. There was help everywhere; but did I want it; would I resist it? That would mean opening up, exposing myself, allowing others to see that I was weak, helpless and needy. Wasn't I, why else had all of this happened in my life?

I walked on "eggshells," attempting to contain the fear and anxiety turning inside me. My little girl repeatedly kept calling for comfort, nurturing and love, yes BIG LOVE.

Then one day I recall, as I walked by a wall mirror, when the pain was beyond unbearable and my heart literally felt broken, I heard a tiny, tiny voice deep inside me say "I love you. You are enough. Ask, just reach out and ask for help." Shaken, I peered deep inside my heart to see possibility and the probability of what was yet to be.

At that moment a "Shift" happened; floodgates opened to release encumbered emotions of shame, guilt, fear, anxiety, anger, and resentment. In flowed Love. Forgiveness was the sweet spot. My life journey became excruciatingly wonderful with a relentless gentle road of Self-Discovery.

Do you know someone named Suzie who may be in danger or desperately need help? One in three women in Canada experiences physical or sexual violence. If you are in crisis, or know someone who is, or need advice, please call your local emergency help line for free, confidential information. Calling 911 will put you in touch with Emergency services or 211 generally for resources.

Check with government and non-government agencies within the community or neighboring community or through schools, colleges, and universities for possible services available or for referrals to other resources. It takes tremendous courage to name the pain. And more to decide enough is enough. You can do it.

Whenever people are abused, they do many different things to oppose the abuse and to keep their self-respect and dignity. Sometimes imagining a better life may be the impetus for Courage to stand up and say, "No more." That may be the deciding moment to walk away from it. If you know someone is being abused let them know you are there for them.

The journey of healing is like the alchemist who mines deeply for coal only to discover the alchemy process has turned it into gold. The journey and awareness are priceless. Before forty, I experienced horrific things in my life. Hitting the wall emotionally crippled me. I could not function. There were days I did not know my name. I became unemployed. I was paralyzed with fear and anxiety. Once I worked through the emotional blocks sometimes weeks, sometimes months, sometimes days, I realized that the experiences were not and are not me. What an empowering feeling this was! I am a better, stronger person because of the difficult situations and from having resisted abuse in so many ways.

Sometimes "shift happens" along the way that affects you. It takes courage to step through; it takes support and love, your love to see you through. The lessons I've learned continuously remind me of the greatness I have inside of me. Just like your lessons can remind you. A life experience is not you. A life experience is just that ... an experience that encourages you to mine for your gold. Don't allow it to rule and run your life. Take the experience, mine the Gold. I learned that it is the catalyst to engage, encourage and empower you to step into bigger and greater areas in your life to be YOU. Be open to the possibilities and turn them into probabilities. There is greatness inside of you. I Believe in You.

Carol masterfully uses her voice to inspire women as they open to their potential and transform their inner strength into Empowered Leadership. Throughout her life, she had her own journey through anxiety, fear, family strife and out-of-balance living. These experiences led her on a quest to discover and unleash her unique voice. Carol is a recognized motivational speaker and International Best-Selling author in Living Without Limitations – 30 Mentors to Rock your World and Your Unique Leader's Voice--A Journey Through Trauma. She is a certified DYBO facilitator, consultant, and mentor, and holds a Master's in Public Administration. As a spiritual entrepreneur, Carol has worked with clients regionally and internationally.

Website: **www.carolmetzmurray.com**

Skype: **carol.metz8.**

Facebook: **facebook.com/busempowerment**

LinkedIn: **linkedin.com/pub/carol-metz-murray**

More Stories to Heal Your World Now

Compiled by Anita Sechesky

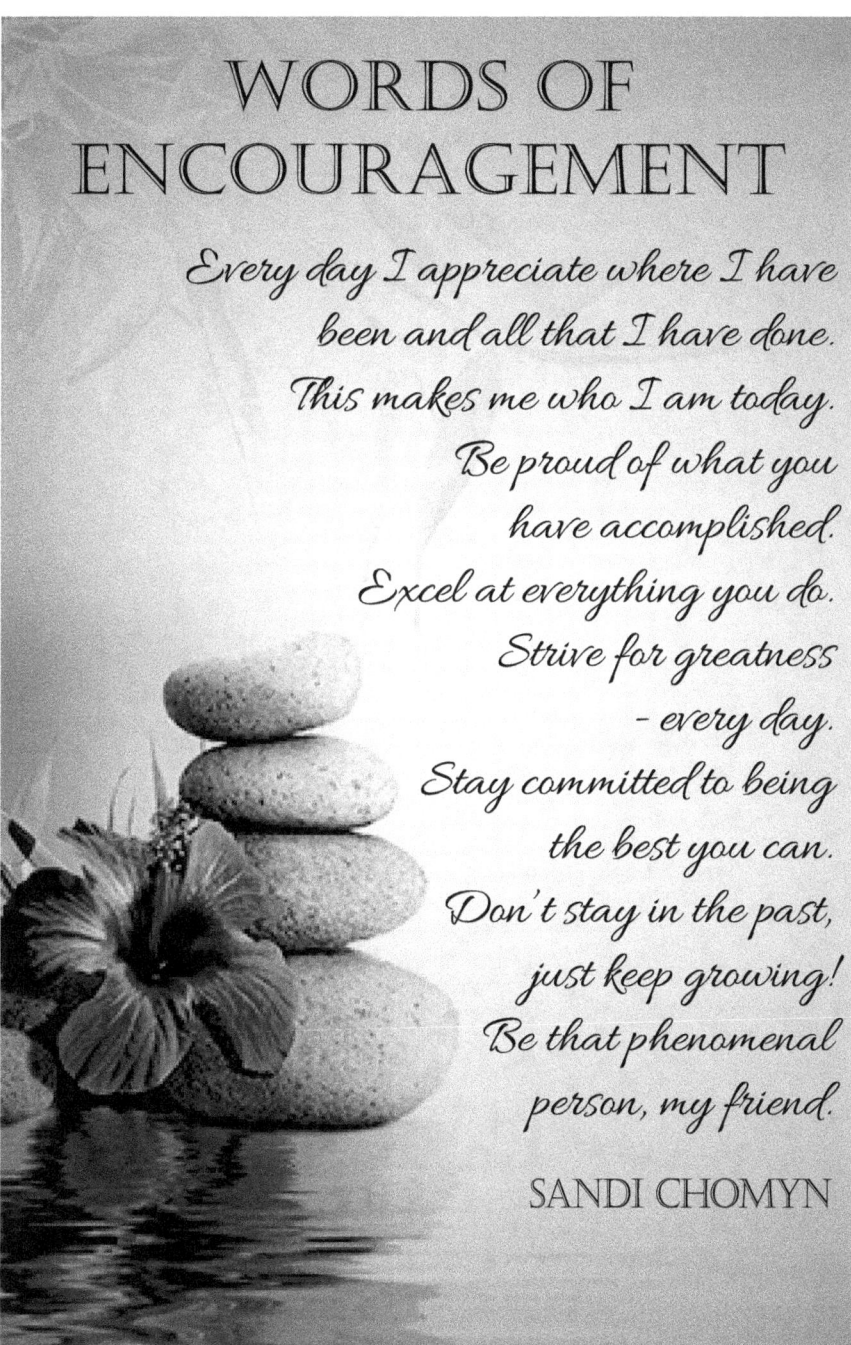

WORDS OF ENCOURAGEMENT

Every day I appreciate where I have been and all that I have done. This makes me who I am today. Be proud of what you have accomplished. Excel at everything you do. Strive for greatness - every day. Stay committed to being the best you can. Don't stay in the past, just keep growing! Be that phenomenal person, my friend.

SANDI CHOMYN

Compiled by Anita Sechesky

CHAPTER THIRTY-ONE

Living in the Fullness of Your Purpose, Passion, and Power

by Kim Thomas

We often hear the term, *"Be the best version of yourself."* The challenge is that we often define being the best as being happy. Happiness, however, is tied to circumstances that are ever-changing and truthfully, always being happy is unrealistic. In fact, being sad, frustrated, and the range of emotions is actually very healthy. What we should seek to be is at peace. You see, peace is not tethered to circumstances; it is a state of mind that is anchored on a core belief system that says regardless of my circumstance, my relationship status, my bank account, my current job, the number of friends I have, or my social media status, I am thankful. Peace is tethered to gratitude and the fact that we are a gift, a miracle, and God's creation. Being the best version of yourself may be the goal, but it first starts with you believing that you are extraordinary because you are created in God's image (Genesis 1:27). And that He has a great plan for your life (Jeremiah 29:11) ~ to live and love with purpose, passion, and power.

Let me establish something first: We are spirit beings. We live in bodies and possess souls. The real person inside us is our spirit. Our soul consists of our mind, will, and emotions. That being said, it's so important for us to acknowledge to be great and live with purpose and power, the work starts within. In today's society, we see value and success portrayed with outer things such as one's position of influence, careers, being popular, looking good, and other material things. Instead, I want us to focus on the following things that are counter-culture to the world's standard of success and power that I believe will catapult you to live your best life.

Vision. You have to have a vision for where you're going ~ which comes from that still, quiet place inside of you that is birthed from God. He uniquely crafted vision and purpose in your life. You don't get your vision from comparing yourself to others. You get your vision from seeking Him and walking in truth. Get around people that will push you towards that vision – those who understand you, cherish you, honor you, and believe in who you are becoming despite your deficiencies or shortcomings. You have to know where you are going and have a plan to get there. Ask God to birth a fresh vision in you. Make sure it aligns with your core values and your passion. Write it down; pray about it daily and find scripture that supports your vision.

Be bold and courageous. Overcome fear with faith. Be intentional about your life. Take action to do more, love more, forgive more, and leave more in this world. Do one small thing every day to move you closer to your dreams and your vision – until they become a reality. A life of excellence is made from small acts of excellence every day. Practice being spectacular long enough and being spectacular will become your default mindset. Your daily consistent behavior truly broadcasts your deepest core values (Joshua 1:9)

Have faith. The faith of the unseen. Faith in the divine. Faith in God. Faith that *"He who began a good work in you will carry it on to completion until the day of Christ Jesus"* Philippians 1:6. Faith that you never walk alone. And faith that the challenges and setbacks that come are not failures, but are designed to move you forward with greater wisdom, power, and resilience. These are chapters in your best-seller book of life. So have faith that God wants the best for you and begin to position yourself to walk in your birthright filled with God's unmerited favor (2 Corinthians 5:7) (Hebrews 11:6).

Be of service. If you're growing just for yourself, and your own satisfaction, approval and ego, you are not growing spiritually. There's a massive difference between being rich and having lots of money and being wealthy where you feel fulfilled and abundant every single day. Our greatest calling is to live a life of service and love towards each other. To leave this world a better place; to be a conduit of God's love ~ His hands extended. To be driven to have impacts and affect change in the world. Along with service comes gratitude. We have more than enough, yet we are often never satisfied. The great call on our lives is to do our part to make others lives better. Make it part of your passion and purpose to serve others and give back to the world more than you take. Be intentional; about giving, generosity, kindness, and servitude.

Be more than a conqueror. I believe one of our downfalls in not living full and victorious lives is that we walk through life like we are powerless (Romans 8:37). We don't claim and walk in our divine calling and the many promises of God. We don't have that warrior mentality like Joshua who was bold and courageous enough to ask God to make the sun stand still to help the Israelites in their battle. We will find our purpose and power when we truly understand that "I can do all things through Christ which strengtheneth me" (Philippians 4:13). Strength is not attained from winning. It is your struggles that develop strength. Success is not built on success; it is built on adversity, setbacks, challenges, and our ability to overcome them. God is greater than the highs and greater than the lows (2 Corinthians 12:9). He is seen in the valley and He is seen at the mountaintop. Indeed, when we acknowledge that God is greater than we can even fathom, and bask in that truth, we can accomplish more.

Seek wisdom and knowledge, then take action. When you know more, you can do more. When you understand more, you can achieve more. Know who you are. We need to come into a place of being before we can come into a place of doing. They say good things come to those who believe, better things come to those who wait, but the BEST things come to those who pursue and never give up. But in doing so, we must seek wisdom through prayer and seek knowledge. Four things we learn from Solomon in the book of Proverbs are: to wake up to reality; define your vision; effectively partner, and finally, pursue wisdom and build your life upon it. Wisdom is also acknowledging that there is a higher power that is working on our behalf. So be smart when pursuing your purpose. We don't have all the answers. See Him who knows us better than we know ourselves (Mark 1:7).

For His glory. God will use whatever you go through for His glory. Nothing happens by coincidence. You were predestined for greatness. Maybe it's not what's happening to you, but what God wants to do through you. Sometimes you will see God through the broken places more than you see Him in the blessed places. Every detour is an opportunity to see the details of your destiny. You have to shift your mindset; every hardship experienced is building you, not breaking you. When you feel you're reaching rock bottom, take refuge because God is the rock at the bottom.

Trust the process. Trust the journey. Know that your best days are still ahead. Know that delay is not denial. Know that you are still becoming. Don't chase money and things, chase purpose.

Our life is ultimately a theatre for personal greatness. Each day is a platform for mastery, a dress rehearsal for success, and a curtain call to give thanks. We lose ourselves to find ourselves. The light transcends the darkness. And may we always shine the spotlight back to God as we acknowledge His ways are higher than our ways (Isaiah 55:9). People often confuse blessings over prosperity. A blessing isn't a thing, but a state of your heart that enables you to be content regardless of your circumstance. Walk in your birthright of blessings. Don't let circumstances steal your joy. Nothing can stop God's plan for your life (Isaiah 14:27). The Lord will personally go ahead of you (Deuteronomy 31:8). He will meet you where you are at, but He won't leave you there.

Be still. Get rid of the clutter and noise. Sometimes we need to get out of our head; stop overthinking and be quiet and still (Psalm 46:10). Seek wisdom and wear it like a crown. In order to have a direction and discipline, you have to be still so you can listen to the great master planner ~ your Creator. It all starts and ends with God at the center of it all, so take time to listen to the plans that He has for your life. We also need to make room for our blessings by removing the clutter and chaos. We have to make a conscious effort to create room for more good in our lives. Make room for more love, compassion, forgiveness, and most importantly, make room for God's presence and to hear His voice. Furthermore, the relationship we have with ourselves will reveal the relationship we have with others.

Surrender. There is indeed a force greater than us. Elohim is one of the first names we see in the Bible that describes God. In Genesis, Elohim is portrayed as the infinite, all-powerful Creator. Rather than persist on God doing something for you, instead, you can rest in what He has already done. You don't have to scheme, manipulate, or beg to make things happen. Believe that it's already done. When you know your birthright in Christ, you can walk in what has already been accomplished for you because you know victory was completed on the cross (Ephesians 2:10). Take courage, for whatever God is going to do for you, He has already done. Whatever God has planned for your life, He has already predestined it. Whatever has been purposed for your life, God has already purposed it. And guess what? It's a good life, one filled with purpose and power, a future and a hope (Jeremiah 29:11). What may have looked like the end for you – a broken relationship, a business failed, a lost loved one, is actually the beginning. When we deny our stories, they define us, but when we surrender to God and own our stories, we get to write the ending. For we know there is someone at work who is greater than us that owns the masterplan, and we design the blueprint.

My relationship with God remains my number one priority. I know that if I take care of that, God will take care of the rest. While I find happiness in the simplest of things, my life is far from perfect. I laugh; I cry; I face disappointment. Sometimes I feel I'm so close, yet so far from where I need to be. But I've come to learn that we often look for God in the destination, but He is found in the detour. That's where you will find Him and learn about yourself ~ In the brokenness, not the blessing. When you're on the detour, Grace will chase you down and love will lead the way. So trust the journey and have faith in the unseen. Stay in His presence. Read His Word. There you will find perfect peace and irreplaceable joy. And this is why I wake up at peace every day ~ thanking God for a right mind and peace of mind.

I want to end by encouraging you that God has a plan for your life today and beyond. (Matthew 7:7-8). Your purpose, passion, and power are fulfilled by walking in your birthright, pursuing your calling, and harnessing your gifts. And it's not always in the public view that God is developing your calling. It's often on the backside of the mountain like David. Be faithful and steadfast in the hidden places where no one else sees. It's not always about doing, but BEING. Being more patient, being more faithful, being more disciplined, being more present, selfless, loving, and kind. It's in the secret place that God develops and elevates you. It's in the quiet mundane moments that you refine yourself. It's in the valley, not the mountaintop, the unseen preparation that catapults you. God is calling you into something that exceeds your limitations, preparing you for something so magnificent that only He can get the credit for. No amount of relational connections or resources can supersede the power of walking in the will of God. What we can labor for in months and years, God can do in a moment. So many people want the platform, but not the process. They want the position, but not the pain. Surrender and trust the process. God's timing is perfect; not ours. Success is not defined by numbers nor achievements, or external validation. Instead, it's your ability to fulfill the will of God, His plan and purpose for your life. Your failures and disappointments have not disqualified you, instead, they have only validated you, and strengthened you. You have cried too many tears, sown too many seeds, celebrated everyone else's success and victories...BUT NOW is your time and I declare that now is YOUR turn to live in the fullness of your purpose, passion, and power!

All bible scripture quotes are taken from the English Standard Version (ESV).

Kim Thomas is a Lifestyle Architect dedicated to helping people move forward in life. Her devotion is to serve, inspire, and encourage. Her mission is to help others achieve personal mastery and transformation. Kim is a speaker, Life and Wellness coach, workshop facilitator and founder of onLIFESTYLEwithkim. A teacher and success coach over twenty years, her extensive background with youth at risk and in the arts as department head, creative director, actor, writer and producer have given her a well-rounded platform. Kim's mantra is to give back to the world more than we take. She is the mother of three extraordinary kids. All glory goes to God.

Facebook: **Kim Thomas**

Instagram: **Kimnthomas**

LinkedIn: **Kimnthomas@gmail.com**

Website: **www.onlifestylewithkim.com**

Email: **kimnthomas@gmail.com**

CHAPTER THIRTY-TWO

Forgiveness: A Vehicle for Self-Transformation & Healing

by Michelle Francis-Smith B.A., RMT

My walk in real forgiveness began in 2015. I was thirty-seven at the time and had lived my life to that point full of great compassion for others, considered by most to be supportive, generous, even forgiving. In 2015, I was also facing some of the biggest and scariest challenges in my career and personal life, and was struggling to understand how and why I had lost my way. When exactly had I turned the corner on myself and given up? It was the work over these next three years that would reveal how much of a blind spot existed for me in true forgiveness.

Most people in my circles would say that I have never been the type to hold grudges. If anything, I encouraged conflict resolution and have been known to turn the other cheek on multiple occasions. So, what could I possibly have to contribute on how to forgive?

In this chapter, I will reveal the secret that I realized was key to unlocking forgiveness and how learning and applying this to my life has transformed my relationship with myself and others, and allowed me to heal in ways I was unaware of.

First, we must go back to those blind spots I mentioned. On my quest to make visible all that lives in my blind spots, I enrolled myself in a self-development program. A main goal in this work is to explore what you don't know that you don't know. We all know what we know and know what we don't know, but our blind spots could also be described as those areas of our existence we don't know that we don't know. With insecurities in toe, I walked into this experience of self-discovery open to the spotlight being shined on those hidden parts of myself. Two areas of my life I was prepared to shake up vigorously: my marriage and my career. Both areas I had experienced huge success and more recent failure, and wanted to understand how and why it all happened. I hoped to grow stronger and protect myself from this defeat ever entering my life again. Take my marriage as a prime example. When I started this self-development program, I was separated from my husband, unsure of how to begin to move on. I absolutely knew I would live and die loving my husband but thought I equally knew that we had outgrown each other and could not function together in a marriage. As for my career, I made a series of mistakes and took responsibility for them which played out in a very public arena. I was facing some extremely broken parts of myself and feeling quite vulnerable and exposed while doing it. The little voice of doubt in my head would regularly say, "How could you have done this to yourself?" "What a disappointment you are!" "This is the end for you…" It was in these darker, quieter spaces I veered into my blind spot. I was horrified to uncover what I did. Through all my successes and accomplishments, I had forgotten a major thing: I never believed I deserved any of it! I had a deep-rooted lack of self-worth which is what was guiding me during my highest points of stress and burnout, and was staring me square in the eye for the first time since childhood. After wrestling with the elements that were coming to light, I realized that the only way to finally put that heavy burden down was to forgive myself for EVERYTHING! The moment this struck me, I chose to stop punishing myself for all of the poor choices I had made. I now understood that any choices I've ever made were based on how the world occurred to me at the time. As a matter of fact, we all make decisions that way. Once I accepted this about myself I could also accept this of others, and with that I WAS SET FREE! Free to forgive, free to love, free to rebuild my integrity for myself and within my relationships. Free to really let go of anger, disappointment and fear, and free to create new possibilities in my life and all the lives I touch. Once the significance of this set in, I was able to recognize how vital self-forgiveness is to experience true forgiveness of others. Circling back to my husband of sixteen years who I had walked away from, I thought I had forgiven and pledged my remorse to. With this newfound awareness I could see that it wasn't at all possible to forgive him and move on from the multiple bumps and bruises we had experienced together, because before becoming acquainted with the baggage within my blind spot, I simply didn't know how.

When you live a life haunted by feeling wronged by others and maintaining a list of offenders who you keep at a distance, you are falsely under the impression that you are protecting yourself from being wronged again. In actuality, you are calling more of the same into your life. Resentment like this is similar to deliberately hitting your head against a brick wall and expecting your enemy to suffer your self-inflicted head trauma. It seems ridiculous but many of us function this way.

I've learned from experience that forgiveness can't change the past, but it can absolutely transform the future. The first step occurs when you grace yourself with enough self-compassion to forgive yourself and facilitate the transformation that comes along with that. It is an exercise in vulnerability when you can get that transparent with YOU, be authentic with YOU, say I love YOU and I forgive YOU! This freedom made possible a cleansing of my career, which is thriving to new heights, and my marriage and I'm proud to say we are standing stronger together today because we both learned how to live in real forgiveness.

Who I am is the possibility of the world healing generationally forward, free of any constraints of the past with the ability to design an amazing future! This has been made possible by walking in real forgiveness. Try it on and experience all that is possible for you!

Michelle Francis-Smith is a mother, entrepreneur, Best-Selling International co-author, mentor, educator, doula, speaker and Registered Massage Therapist since 2001. She is excited to compile an Anthology entitled *You Have So Much Potential: Inspiring Healing in Your Clients' Transformation*, which is set to be released in 2018 with LWL PUBLISHING HOUSE!

CHAPTER THIRTY-THREE

Nourishing My Soul
by Natalie Bélair

One beautiful Sunday morning, I was listening to some soothing chanting music and saw the amazing sunlight shining bright and beaming through my living room window.

My heart was smiling, opened and full of joy as I embrace the beauty and nurtured my beloved plants. I turn to speak and smell my favorite plant, the peace lily, as I looked to see if she had roots that needed to be pulled.

She then proceeded to whisper these beautiful but powerful words of wisdom:

> *You see my love, plants are like people. We all need to be loved and nurtured in different ways. Some need to be watered more frequently; others require their leaves massaged or fluffed, smelled, beautified, cleansed, or given attention, love, nutrients, and valued, appreciated, and de-rooted.*
>
> *At times, you will find dead roots or leaves that simply need to be picked up. There will be times where the dead roots are still well grounded in the plant and don't want to be removed. Other times, you will have to gently pull the ones that need help in detaching, releasing, and letting go in order to create the space for the plant to continuously flourish and grow.*

Taking a moment to embrace the wisdom, I'm in awe and have an "aha moment." It's so true! The soul of the plant has enlightened me with a beautiful gift. "We are not all the same," I say to myself, glancing at the other plants and flowers in my living room.

It is important to love, appreciate, and respect one's individual needs knowing we all require love and nurturing in different ways. It is also equally important to understand our authenticity and functioning of who we are in our own relationship with one's self. In doing so, we are able to determine how our soul needs to be nourished to grow.

I can personally relate to the roots of this plant's soul. Most of my life I wore the mask of the people pleaser. I really thought that's what it meant to be loved as I did not really know what love felt like. For me, it was all about making others happy and by serving them, it made me happy. Or so I thought!

In 2012, through forced life experiences and lessons, I quickly came to the realization that I did not know who I was anymore. I only knew how to be a mother. Even then I felt guilty, judged and ashamed, and always compared myself to the "perfect mothers" who came along my path.

I then asked the question: *Who are you?*

My answer was, well, umm...let's see...I am a mother of four. I've been a mom for seventeen years and umm...

Dead silence! Whew...I got nothing else. I am a mother!

Yes, that I know. *What else? Who am I?*

Standing there in silence with no clue of who I was, confused with a puzzled look on my face, I kept asking myself.

- What do I love?
- What is my passion?
- What brings me joy?
- What makes my heart smile?
- What are my fears?
- Who am I?

Like the plant, *how do I get my nectar? How do I nourish and flourish my juicy soul?*

One step at a time, moment by moment the journey in seeking my identity and self-discovery began.

I quickly realized fear was my biggest emotion that consumed my world, therefore, I decided to slowly face it and start there.

What was I afraid of doing by myself?

What steps do I require to lean into my balance of authenticity?

Here comes dating myself 101 beloved souls and how I learned to embrace and empower my Yin feminine energies by balancing my emotional and soul bodies and freeing my inner child as I discovered my authentic self.

Step one for me was learning self-love and to appreciate myself.

I started simply by buying myself flowers; I always loved receiving them but had forgotten how it felt like. The simple act of appreciating myself with this modest yet easy gesture brought me to a mindful state. I deserve these beautiful flowers for I am a flourishing seed within which desperately craves growth and freedom.

I then started to feel my heart smiling and opening up again. Oh wow...what a feeling!

As I continued in the flow and feeling this simple love for myself, I had to respect my limited financial budget. It did not always permit me, therefore, I learned to be creative.

Once a month I made it a priority to purchase a big beautiful bouquet of flowers that spoke to me at that moment. I then would excitedly head home to make myself many little bouquets and was inspired to write little love notes.

I smiled from ear to ear at that very moment. I inhaled and exhaled, taking a moment to appreciate the profound love I was giving myself. I spread these tiny self-made bouquets of joy with my positive love messages about myself all over the house. I then learned to embrace every moment to stop, smell, inhale, appreciate, and read the love deep within.

I then felt inspired to move forward with my step number two: *Dating myself.*

I realized that I was afraid to venture out to a restaurant by myself and no, I'm not talking about fast foods, dear soul reading this. I am talking about an actual sit-in dining lounge; here was where the fear would kick in with me sitting there all alone as the server approached me to remove the extra place settings on the table that was lovingly designed for two.

Whew...yes that's right! Not so easy for me. However, I decided to be gentle with myself and respected my comfort zone by leaning into the side and my emotions of fear. I decided to take it step by step and go at lunchtime as I clearly knew there would be fewer people watching and judging me.

I chuckle to myself as I look back now. *I was the one living in fear and judging myself all along.*

The proudest feeling though (of conquering that fear and taking myself on my first date) still resides deep within me today. The deepest gratitude, love, and compassion for myself was starting to settle in.

I enjoyed the learning process of dating myself that I continue to explore this. I would sit in coffee shops for hours in a mindful state. Then I preceded to go to the cinema and watch movies that I wanted to see. Wink...I was in awe and fell in love with the idea of being able to enjoy a movie of my choice without pleasing anyone else.

So on and so forth, my blessed and guided adventures continued as I explored and traveled the world. After five years, I was so tired of waiting for someone to travel with that I took a leap of faith and continued my self-discovery to other countries. These travel dates took me to dreams and places in different dimensions, magical and proud moments, doors of opportunities, and truly living a lifestyle without limitations.

In honor of my Love and Gratitude, I started to leave myself love notes filled with compliments and even thanked myself for the lovely dates in my bouquets of flowers. Hahaha...why not?

This led me to continue my journey of moving forward to step number three: *Self-Care*

Oh yes! The feeling of bliss. At this point, I started to fall in love with myself though I noticed that I was neglecting my outer beauty as well. Pamper me, here we come. Yeah for me!

Now I was to discover what that meant for me. Keep in mind my budget was limited, therefore, I continued to be creative. I would love to go to the spa, I said to myself, but this was not cost-efficient at the time. My creative light came on and decided to not let that stop me.

I googled *do it yourself organic spa treatments*. I am grateful for Google, let me tell you. My inner child was coming out to play. Yeah! I was making different facial masks, body lotions, exfoliates, bath salts and even tried to make some do it yourself make-up. I was doing my manicures and pedicures, enjoying candlelight bubble baths and soul dancing.

It was a trial and error for me. Some I preferred more than others, however, I learned to appreciate the journey. I was re-discovering my inner child by permitting myself to have fun, play, and explore. I was choosing to free her and not wear the mommy or wife mask in order to nurture her.

As my self-care journey continued to flourish and grow, I was mindful of the products I was putting on and in my body. I became more conscious of the importance of the nutrients my soul was absorbing, both inside and out. That alone was a journey which continues to flourish to this day.

From there, I became a vegetarian and tip-toed with vegan meals. My self-care also included discovering what my body needed. My body was not hesitating of telling me what its likes and dislikes were, as I tapped into my Divine gifts of being an empath. Don't get me wrong, I do love my potato chips, however, my body does not always agree. I was feeling every single energetic sensation around and within me, which led me to explore deeper within the healing of my soul and my inner child.

Next came the fourth and last step: *Gratitude & Balance*

Listening to my guidance and intuition is a journey in itself, however, I learned to navigate towards what resonates deep within my soul and screams for my inner child to be set free.

From my personal experiences, spiritual groups, healing tools, and teachings, it was important for me to be grateful and to recognize, observe, acknowledge, take responsibility, let go a.k.a. surrender, and make choices as to what my inner child needs to learn.

As I balance my yin and yang despite the chatter around me, I became my empowered Goddess within!

As I stand there in the space I created and grounded in my truth, I find myself with the deep power of enlightenment and profound inner wisdom of my planted roots from all lifetimes.

I appreciate, embrace, and welcome with gratitude the beautiful souls along my path (as I now see them as my mirror) and doors of opportunities to understand the underlying gifts to liberate my soul to freedom.

Gratitude and balance are my keys to my authenticity!

I can now say with affirmation that my little woman inside is grounded, confident, fierce, emotional, energetic, fun, loving, romantic, creative, filled with laughter, adventurous, spontaneous, playful, and was screaming to come out and discover the beauty of all. She now has created her own space to exist, be heard, seen, and nurtured in a fun, loving, soft, gentle, kind, and compassionate way. She continues to be liberated one step at a time.

Countless bow downs my beloved plant for your truth, wisdom, inner and outer beauty.

Why not give yourself the greatest gift of opening your heart further to see the beauty and free your inner child to an unlimited explosion of authentic love?

- How do you nourish your soul?
- What are your steps to self-discovery?
- What are your self-care tools?
- How do you free your inner child?

As I connect, heart to heart and soul to soul with you, I truly feel blessed and honored to be able to share my personal journey with you of how I nourish my soul.

In closing, I would like to give my gratitude to my heaven's team, all the teachers along my journey, countless bow downs to the Divine with continuous love and gratitude flowing to all.

I am forever grateful!

Love & Light

 Natalie Bélair was born and raised in Timmins, Ontario and currently lives in Ottawa. She is an International Best-Selling Author and Owner of Angelic Changes. Natalie is a Certified Intuitive Energy & Soul Healer, Spiritual Teacher, Soul Communicator, Inspirational Speaker, and Road Block Destroyer with over eighteen years' experience in medical management. She uses a heart-centered "Soul Song" to remove soul, mind, emotional, and body blockages to transform all aspects of life, both in the present and past lifetimes. Her mission is to be an Unconditional Servant, spreading love, peace, harmony and to shine her light as brightly as possible.

Facebook: **www.facebook.com/IntuitiveEnergySoulHealing**

Website: **http://angelicchanges.com/**

More Stories to Heal Your World Now

Compiled by Anita Sechesky

WORDS OF ENCOURAGEMENT

After conquering cancer Twice, I can say that mindset plays a massive role in how we experience life and how we heal. Focus on the good health you desire, Not the illness that you don't!

Your obstacles in life can paralyze you or propel you forward.

SARAH D. BAILEY

More Stories to Heal Your World Now

Compiled by Anita Sechesky

CHAPTER THIRTY-FOUR

How We as Parents Can Connect with Our Daughters

by Sharon Ann Marie Stewart

As an educator, mentor, and coach, I have been blessed over the last forty years to have worked with some amazing girls and young women. I have been able to witness all of their ages and stages: the puberty fiascos, the brain transitions, and the growth of them into beautifully spirited young women.

I have also been able to witness these same youthful beautiful spirits grow into young women and then women, who are feeling misunderstood and confused about who they are in the world presently. They have grown into women, each with a little girl still inside, who were never able to fully develop or let go of childhood issues.

You see, as children or little girls, they all had this tremendous desire to be seen and heard. Not with normal foolish childish antics or play, but heard in regards to how they felt. They, like many of us, were often quieted or limited to what it was that they were able to communicate to their parents. They were shut down or given very little space to express their feelings. When they were given the chance to speak, they weren't believed when they spoke about matters that meant a lot to them – an experience some of us know all too well.

I can vividly remember wanting to ask my own mother questions about things like how my body was changing or something I heard said out in the playground at school and I didn't really understand. She would always get annoyed with me and tell me to go read a book or go play. Poor thing. To her and other mothers' defense, this was the way they grew up.

They were raised at a time when you were not to ask things that would make others uncomfortable or what would be deemed inappropriate for a girl child to ask. My poor mother would blush and become so embarrassed that her daughter would speak of such things and then be irritated for the rest of the day. For me, that was horrible because I learned as a child that you were to dismiss or shut down any feelings that you may want to share. Children were to be seen and not heard.

A child who is not able to express their feelings does not acquire a strong emotional foundation. They do not develop the capacity to use language to communicate properly and in turn, the lack of emotions affects the way they think, decide, and solve problems, leading to inappropriate feelings of guilt, shame, and embarrassment.

Unfortunately, as a result of that dismissive behavior and lack of expression, we now have generations of women who have developed emotionally impaired thinking; women who are now afraid to speak and are being misguided by guilt, shame and other emotional deficiencies that allow them to make decisions that do not positively serve them.

Examples of such are women staying in unhealthy relationships, not using their power of yes or no to create lifestyles of openness and freedom.

We, as parents, now need to revamp this old way of thinking and step out of our comfort zones in order to help our daughters grow emotionally sound.

Here is a list of five tested and proven strategies that will allow you to connect better with your daughter(s).

Number One

Listen. It's the MOST important thing we can do.

Here's what normally happens: your daughter comes to speak with you about an issue she has, something SHE wants to discuss. You, as the great parent, find it your job as the elder to use this chance to finally tell her everything you've ever done. We automatically become a classroom instructor, always trying to teach her a lesson or reminding her what to do or not to do. This would all great if that's what she came to you for...but it wasn't.

To her dismay, we still keep going on with the lecture. We have all heard it before from our parents and we just continue the legacy. "When I was your age this, and when I was your age that." "Blah, blah, blah." Sound familiar? We become immensely emotional. We begin to get lost in our own moment and begin thinking about the things that happened to us or we create delusional thoughts, like our children may be more advanced than we were or whatever crazy thoughts go through our minds at that time.

This is a one-way conversation where we are left feeling amazing or distressed. Some of us even pat ourselves on our back for a great talk, as we got everything off our chests and we feel like the best teachers ever...but your daughter – remember her? – is left with the unanswered question and the emotional void.

Here's what we **NEED** to do:

Stop talking and let her speak. Let her express whatever it is she wants to say. Stop talking and listen. Do the head nod or the bobblehead, whatever will let her know you are listening. Be nonjudgmental. She may tell you something that will blow your mind.

Do not interrupt until she is finished...which may take hours, but let her speak all the way until the record starts to skip. This will teach her that she is okay to express herself and that her voice matters.

Number Two

Spend quality time with your daughter.

This is a huge, huge, huge – did I say HUGE – way for parents to connect with their daughters. The more time that you take to spend with your daughter or daughters, the more you will be able to build a relationship with them.

From a mother's standpoint: this is perfect. It is a beautiful way to listen and be involved in their daily lives while doing an activity you are all enjoying.

While you are appreciating your quality time, you begin to see her regular patterns and habits. This will allow you to notice when things become different with her. You will become aware of behavioral and emotional changes quicker, helping you to investigate and intercept problems before it may be too late.

From a daughter's standpoint: she gets to develop a comfortable relationship with you. This will help her to freely talk to you without feeling the pressure of approaching you. It will be safe, fun, and natural. What better way to have a solid connection with your mother?

Number Three

Be present.

Often times, as life would have it, we are engaged in many activities or conversations, trying to multitask. Cooking, cleaning, returning texts, reading emails, and talking on the phone.

When your daughter is trying to connect with you, STOP EVERYTHING AND BE PRESENT.

In that moment, your daughter needs to know that she is most important. She needs to feel that what she is about to say will be heard and not buried with "Uh huh" "Sorry" "Hold on" "What did you say?" This is her time and she deserves that moment all to herself without any interruptions.

They need to see you put the phone down, invite them to a nice comfortable space, turn the stove lower, or close the laptop. Also, hug them, rub their foreheads, give some form of physical touch so that they may feel super safe and wanted. This is her moment. Be present.

Number Four

Realize that they are NOT you.

I have seen so many women or friends of mine come to the conclusion that their past mistakes will be that of their daughters. They somehow fear that what they did foolishly in the past will resurface in their daughters.

Most often, it is not our past behaviors but what we are presently modeling for them that they tend to repeat. Nonetheless, when she comes to you with an issue or just the need to express, remove all possible negative thoughts or feelings that may surface and remember that she is not you.

We need to let our daughter be themselves and not to try to create a newer version of our old self. We need to step away from any feeling that we may have and repeat, repeat, repeat that she is NOT you.

Number Five

Be HONEST

When I say be honest, I mean be just that. You want to let your daughter know that you too were once a child or teenager and had similar thoughts or feelings. Again, you are not making it about you or putting your fears on them, but you are showing her that what is happening may have happened to you or others you may know as well.

When you tell your story, tell it in such a way that will show you have overcome or defeated it. This will create the feeling that she too is not alone and will get through it with the help you will offer along the passing of time.

If it is a serious issue and you cannot handle it alone, tell her that and invite others that you both trust to help. Let her see you as human and vulnerable just like she is.

Now, I am in no way saying that this going to be super easy or that everyone will have the perfect cookie cutter situation. We are all human. As parents, we come to the table with our own baggage from the past – our own personal hurts and fears.

We now have daughters and the cycle of our mothers and their mothers and their mother's needs to be released. It needs to stop here. We need to create a healthy and safe environment for our daughters to come to us when they are scared or have questions.

Let me leave you with this, a simplified version of what I just spoke about. Whenever your daughter wants to connect or talk with you...just SMILE.

    S - Stop what you're doing

    M - Make a nonjudgmental space

    I - Invite her in with a physical touch and open conversation

    L - Listen...DO NOT interrupt

    E - Enjoy the moment

Let's connect with our daughters and create a new generation of women who have a solid emotional foundation and are not afraid of expressing themselves.

A motivator, mother, educator, roadblock destroyer, and lover of life, Sharon Ann Marie Stewart is an inspiring force on a mission to help young girls and women discover the power of themselves. Her desire to be the voice for the silent and the strength of the weak led her to become the founder and president of Simply Anew Me, a non- profit organization. Sharon will be sharing her stories of rebirth and renewal in her new anthology *Healing the Little Woman Inside* later this year.

Compiled by Anita Sechesky

CHAPTER THIRTY-FIVE

Grief to Grow Through
by Stephanie Roy

When my little sister and my best friend passed away four years ago at thirty-eight years of age, leaving behind two young children, I thought nothing could be worse. But watching her wither away in her last months I realized there was something almost as unbearable – survivor guilt.

For those not familiar with the psychological term, it's the feeling that it should have been you instead – not your loved one who should have been taken. It's even worse when you have a disease yourself that makes you a walking time bomb, never sure when you will expire.

You see, Josee was born with throat polyps that stopped her breathing when she was young, so she had a tracheotomy put in as a child and had it most of her life. Although she went through her own issues growing up, mostly social, we were told by the doctors that she would lead an ordinary, typically long life.

I grew up normal, at first glance, but it wasn't until I was twenty-three that a severe congenital heart disease was discovered when I had an unexpected aortic aneurysm. When I woke up from an intense emergency open-heart surgery, I was told that I had a condition that made my aortic tissue weak which caused a pinhole. Although I felt amazing afterward, I was told I had a higher chance of developing another one eventually, therefore shortening my lifespan significantly.

So, I guess it was because we both understood how short life was, we had a love of life that actually brought me and my sister closer together. We learned that life was too short to waste on negativity. Death was always something that happened to other people. It was never taken seriously. We used to joke together about who would go first.

As we got older, life happened as it usually does, and my sister had a family with two beautiful children. Because of my heart condition, I was told not to have any, so I instead delighted in the company of my niece and nephew. Life was good.

We enjoyed life to the fullest, together usually, except for one small difference. Because I never had the chance to have children, which was a life goal since I was a child myself, I lived a very reckless lifestyle. I felt I had nothing to lose. I drove my car like I was driving through the gates of Hell itself and got into numerous accidents... always leaving without a scratch. I hung around with the most dangerous people and saw things no woman or man should ever have to see. I've been beat almost to death and had many partners over the years with no regard for my safety most of the time. I treated life like it was a dare, and after every close call, I would laugh in the face of God, almost gloating and saying, "Ha! Missed me again!" I felt I was invincible.

Then came the day of the dreaded diagnosis of my sweet sister. The shock and denial were expected I guess, but it was the anger stage that for me was the most profound. I went through a stage where I hated God. I never doubted the existence of a Higher Being. I just thought if he did exist, he must be a real jerk, or worse. I mean seriously, how could he take my sister while other people were allowed to live on?

This, of course, prompted the big question: How was I allowed to live? I wasn't exactly a God-fearing person, mind you neither was my sister, but I believe it's been established that I may have had a little less respect. I had no children, and don't get me wrong, I had a huge network of friends and family who would have missed me terribly, but they would go on. Kids need a mom. This made me even angrier, and of course, this is what started the survivor guilt. I felt devastated that I would still be here even after she was gone. It just wasn't fair. I felt I was paying the price for my pride.

I was in absolute wretched misery. It wasn't until months after she passed away that I realized I had to get out of this rut of self-pity. I was tired of thinking the world would be better off without me. So the question of the day was: How do you beat survivor guilt?

I began to look at it logically. I had always felt invincible, but that was a fallacy; eventually, I was going to die too just like everyone else. I may have somehow held it off for a while, but it wouldn't last forever. I was no more special than anyone else and I had just accepted that. Once I recognized I was just like everyone else, I had to think of a way to somehow make my sister immortal.

It was my sister herself who solved that problem without realizing it. During her final days at the hospice, she told me about a journal she had written in her last six months, about her experience with cancer. Her final wish to me was to find that journal, read it, and finish it with my part about how we grew up as sisters. She wanted me to write a book about our life experiences, good and bad, and then get it published. I, of course, couldn't say no. But it wasn't until I started writing that I actually felt better about my guilt, and I realized why. First of all, logic kicked in saying it was impossible to blame her cancer on myself. That was an unfortunate life event that I had no control over, and that's important to realize. You have no control over death! Look around...good people die all the time, along with survivors. Bad people die too. Death doesn't discriminate – it's random.

But it was more than that. All my life I had wondered about immortality and now thanks to her journal, she was actually going to be immortal in the minds of others by keeping her memory alive. Maybe she could actually help someone who was going through the same thing while reading the book. I was going to make sure her death was not in vain.

It's also therapeutic to keep a little personal ritual as a reminder. For example, my sister, my brother, and I had a little ritual when we went out. We always hung out together and we would start every night with a shot of tequila. So, now every year on her birthday, me and everyone who ever knew her have a shot of tequila in her honor, no matter where we are, and then post it on Facebook. Seeing how much love and support she had throughout her life always reminds me of how she will truly never be forgotten.

And as for my past reckless behavior, meh, I'm getting too old for that now. Those days are done. Now I can relax and be a normal person...well mostly (wink wink). But never think for a second that I regret anything I ever did. If staying the same person I am today meant I would have to go back and do it all over again the same, I wouldn't even hesitate. I would do it again in a heartbeat.

So, what's the best way to beat survivor guilt? Remind yourself that you are not responsible for a loved one's death. You are here for a reason. Don't let it go to waste. I'm still here, like it or not. And that's just the randomness of life. Don't beat yourself about it. If that person could see you, they would only want the best for you and to be happy. I know I would if the roles were reversed. Besides, as cliché as it sounds, you never know when your number's up. I am reminded of the time I was walking into the hospital in my twenties. I saw this ancient old man in a wheelchair struggling to push his wheels so he could get through the door. I, of course, dropped everything and helped him. After he was inside, he looked up at me with this feeble smile and said, "You know, all my life I took immaculate care of myself. I worked hard, I didn't smoke, ate well, exercised, didn't drink, and didn't smoke. And look at how I get paid back for that. You want my advice? Do everything you can and don't waste a second because a quick death would have been much better than this." They are words I never forgot.

As for my feelings about God, I think we've come to some uneasy terms. We're good now, but I'm still not going to church.

I think the most important way to get over survivor guilt though is to let those special people live on through others. Write a book about them or a memoriam. Make sure they are not forgotten. Trust me, you will get closure from this. The feeling that you can help someone through something as tragic as this feels like it wasn't wasted. Don't let them be forgotten, even by themselves. In other words, if that person could see you now, would they be proud that you did not let them pass away in obscurity? And of course, take advantage of the life you were given. Don't piss it away. Life was meant to be lived and appreciated. Love yourself always. Love life.

Stephanie Roy is an aspiring author who graduated from Algoma University in 2011 with a BA in Psychology and a Minor in English Literature. Her goal is to understand human nature and has been trying to accomplish this endeavor by being employed in as many different occupations as possible including taxi driver, carnival worker, actress, and youth worker in high risk areas. Stephanie currently resides in Montreal, Quebec with her dog Sadie, and is working on an autobiography about her sister who passed away from cancer, and the impact this disease leaves behind for families and loved ones.

CHAPTER THIRTY-SIX

Social Media: The Magic behind the Personal Branding Tools for Everyone

by Sujit K. Reddy

The world has seen so much fast-paced movement in all aspects of technology, specifically in the last 100 years. Within those 100 years, the past fifteen years has moved even quicker with the advent of Social Media.

Social Media has taken the world over in a very real way. The majority of humanity has been affected by it either directly or indirectly in 2018. It has become a part of the Global Village, and almost part of the "citizenship package" that one receives when being born into the world.

Let me clarify this a bit with an incident that I was witness to recently. I was in a branch of a local telecommunications company to pay my cell phone bill. While I was in line, I was observing a baby held in its mothers' arms was reaching over the mother's arms to play with a tablet. Even though the tablet didn't have any power connected to it, the baby knew enough to make a "swipe" motion on the screen to get things going! I was blown away. The mother noticed I was observing this, confirmed that the baby was almost two years old, had access to a tablet at home, and could operate it all on his own to do with it what he wanted and needed! Imagine that!

I have been a Human Resources Professional since 2001, and as a result, have had the unique privilege of seeing the beginnings of social media, how it has become a part of many workplace cultures, and how some employees have a better time with using it to their benefit, versus other employees who get caught up in it to their determent.

There are a few examples I can recall, one specific, and one not so specific, to illustrate this point. The first was an incident that occurred fairly early on in my corporate HR career. I was working for a well-known Canadian bank at that time, and our Employee Relations department was made aware of a situation in which an employee decided to take some racy pics of themselves and post them on social media. That was not the problem though. The issue was that the bank's logo could be seen in the background. So, needless to say, that employee had to take those pictures down and was disciplined accordingly.

The not so specific incident involves potential candidates for available jobs in any organization. Most recruiters these days, as part of their personal due diligence, will google you. So, for example, if you have videos or pictures of you and your friends partying on the weekend in not so flattering poses or positions because you are under the influence of some substance perhaps, searchable on social media, then this might go against your character. Now, some people may view this as "unfair," but I ask you to pause for a moment and think about it from the company's perspective, with respect to the position they are asking you to take on. Often, you are required to represent your company when you are at work and that company has a certain image and brand to protect which, as their employee, you need to be in alignment with, online and offline.

A way to ensure that you are looking like the most ideal employee before taking on a new job and while you are employed in a position is quite simply to manage your personal brand on social media.

This is not easy, nor is it simple. You have to really pay attention to the small details. For example, recruiters often browse for available candidates on LinkedIn©. Now, if you are someone who goes on your phone while you are on the bus, or when you are bored, and fills out profiles half way and then leaves them like that, thinking: "No one bothers to check this!" "It doesn't really make a difference!" I am here to tell you that it does! As a recruiter, one of my biggest pet peeves has been people who do up their social media profiles, and do not bother to put up their picture in the spot where one is supposed to go! Now, people may say "But it shouldn't matter what I look like in order to qualify for a job that requires my knowledge and skills!" You would be right about that, but this simple oversight is not about that! It is about your attention to detail and how much you care about how others perceive you! By not including a profile picture, it is like walking into an interview with a paper bag over your head!

As the globe is becoming closer because of social media, and more generations are searching for their place in the work world, we have a responsibility to ensure our personal brands online truly reflects who and what we are. This may require us to google ourselves from time to time, ensuring nothing is out on the internet that we do not want to be. If you do find something you don't like, consult with your closest techie friend to figure out how to get it removed, if you yourself can't seem to get it done. Another thing we can do is to teach the youngest of us how to brand themselves better on social media and what to do and not do on these amazing free tools of personal branding.

In closing, it is my hope that you have felt like you have come away with tips and strategies for yourselves or to even advise others on how to heal from the wrong social media moves, personally and professionally, by rebranding yourself and showing that you match your online brand in the office place as well!

Sujit K. Reddy excels at everything his sets his mind to. He is a seasoned HR Professional who has had more than a decade of experience in influential roles that include working with three Canadian Financial Institutions (i.e., RBC, TD, and Scotiabank). Sujit runs his own HR consulting firm known as Human Capital Solutions. He is a seasoned speaker whose various topics use life experiences for all types of audiences. Sujit enjoys spending his free time traveling locally and internationally. Throughout his life, he has sought to make the world a better place.

Website: **www.sujitspeaks.com**

Email: **bookings@sujitspeaks.com**

Facebook: **facebook.com/THESujitK.Reddy**

Twitter: **twitter.com/SujitSpeaks**

LinkedIn: **linkedin.com/in/sujitkreddy**

CHAPTER THIRTY-SEVEN

Inspiration Comes from Our History and Determines Our Future!

by Anita Sechesky

Inspiration only comes when we remember that nothing is determined by the value others place on us. Inspiration comes from the ones in our lives who could have given up so long ago, when others spoke things that could have been our fate.

Inspiration comes from when we see the helpless who have overcome when they had nothing.

Inspiration comes from the wounds that you carry deep inside of you that no one else can see.

Inspiration comes from these wounds that slowly bled for days, months and even years until one day you realized that you and only you could help those wounds to get the help and care they need to truly heal.

Inspiration comes even after losing your first child who had given you dreams to fulfill and plans to make. Inspiration and healing come slowly when you can hear your second baby, a newborn baby boy, cry and coo as you look down into your arms and feel the love of the whole Universe in your grasp that you are a mother again and this time you are feeling the emotions in living color. Inspiration comes when God blesses you again with another beautiful son, your dreams are alive, and they are blessed! God is a good God and as his child, he will find ways to bless you when you least expect it, and in the most amazing and wonderful of ways.

Inspiration comes even after you have been told the most hurtful, degrading and spiteful things you would never imagine being told to any other human being, you hang your head down for a brief moment and realize that your will to survive is greater and stronger, and when God and your loved ones are on your side, you have nothing to lose.

Inspiration comes when you have a moment of weakness and cannot take the verbal, mental and damaging abuse from people you respect...thoughts of hopelessness and despair flood your intellect, and you are on the edge, ready to throw it all away once and for all...then all of a sudden you have a vision and see that sweet, innocent, beautiful, precious little face looking at you and realize. Life has only just begun!

Inspiration comes to you when you least expect it...when you realize you have a purpose and no matter what anyone has ever said, done or treated you. You are better than all of that! When you realize that the way people treat one another is only a reflection of what is going on in their world and they are projecting their values and beliefs on you based on their own sad limiting beliefs.

Inspiration comes from the simple pat on the back from a friend or stranger when you have just decided that you cannot do this any longer without confirmation that you're on the right track.

Inspiration comes from the stories of a Grandma who was a widow from the tender age of twenty-eight with eight children, consisting of the eldest being one set of ten-year-old twins and the two youngest were still in diapers, one of whom is your father. Inspiration comes from remembering Grandma only had a grade school education and was given away to live with her in-laws at the precious age of 9 years old. Inspiration comes from hearing how she had no choice but to work after losing my Grandfather, the love of her life.

Inspiration comes in waves when you hear how she had to labor in a rice and cane field with swampy waters and how she was terrified of snakes but had no choice and had to go work. Inspiration comes when I think of how she was offered to be re-married many times and always said, "No" because of how much she loved her children and did not want her family to be separated. Inspiration comes when I think how my Grandma managed to keep and maintain a large piece of land with fruit and vegetable plantations for her children, all by herself.

Inspiration comes to me and fills my heart once more when I remember this conversation with my late sweet Grandma, "Ma, I feel like I don't fit in." "It doesn't matter if you don't fit in...I don't fit in." my Grandma told me on her hospital bed. "Ma, I don't think they really care about me." "It doesn't matter if they don't love you! I love you and Jesus Loves you" my beloved Grandma whispered to me through her pain." Ohhh, how I wished I had crawled into her hospital bed and held her close like she did to me as a child, but I had just finished working and still had on my scrubs and did not want to soil her bed. It was the last time she told me those words before she passed to be reunited with the love of her life my Grandfather who had passed so many years before. I will never forget her love and words of inspiration to me and all of her loved ones over the years.

Inspiration comes from having a mom who was raised by a step-mother, who was abusive and neglectful, and a father who was absent and an alcoholic. Inspiration comes from hearing your own story of how your mom's pregnancy with you was almost terminated so many times and she had to have blood transfusions and was hospitalized to carry you to full term.

Inspiration comes from hearing the story of being a toddler and your parents were told that as a young child with Gastro in South America. Your chances of survival were next to none, even after being seen by four Paediatricians/Doctors and treated and they had given up informing my parents they should be planning a service. But then understanding that your young parents who loved you so much decided to take turns reading the Bible out loud all night over you while you were sleeping and through their faith and dedication you survived and amazed the doctors.

Inspiration comes and changes everything it can and will change your destiny if you let it! It can be when a stranger believes in you. God and the Universe set it up, and all that was once negative, discouraging, and damaging has now been replaced by all that is positive, encouraging, and beautiful!

There is hope for all that are hopeless! There is strength for the weak! There is love for the unloved, and there is a place in the heart of those who are compassionate and full of mercy and grace for those who are in need.

Inspiration comes from life all around us. Yes, when I hear the things others have gone through I realize I have a lot to be "Thankful for" and recognize it's time to give back! Inspiration is all around us. Are you looking? Are you appreciating? Are you grateful?

Inspiration comes from looking past your current situation, seeing what else is out there, how much others need your seeds of hope, and to know and understand their value.

Inspiration is the foundation of a Life without Limitations. ~

These are bits and pieces of my life story. What is yours?

We all have one. Check yours and see where you were and where you are now. The future never looked brighter! ~

God Bless each and every one of you!

Anita Sechesky

Anita is the Brampton Chapter President of the Holistic Chamber of Commerce because she believes in supporting all entrepreneurs who work from a mind, body & spirit perspective. As a Registered Nurse with over twenty years in Health Care, she has worked with all age groups and diversities.

Anita has excellent written, and communication skills is empathetic and goal-oriented. She is as an ICF - Certified Professional Coach, Publisher, Law of Attraction Practitioner, and soon-to-be Master of NLP Practitioner, as well as a #1 and multiple Best-Selling author.

Email: **lwlclienthelp@gmail.com**

Website: **www.lwlpublishinghouse.com**

CHAPTER THIRTY-EIGHT

Embracing Your EQ and Weakened Areas
by Anita Sechesky

IQ - Your learned information/knowledge inventory

EQ or EI - Your personal/emotional response and behavioural inventory

Did you know that if you are a Leader or CEO of your company, it is a powerful tool to understand and examine what your weak areas of emotional intelligence are?

i4cp found that only about a quarter of companies with 1,000 or more employees have implemented an emotional intelligence initiative in parts of their organization...two-thirds of high-performing organizations apply the concept to their executives. But fewer than half of the low-performing organizations do so.

In this study, emotional intelligence was defined as the degree to which a person has the ability to recognize and understand emotions and the skills to manage personal, individual, and team performance using such awareness.

Interestingly enough... "were more likely to focus EI initiatives on leadership development than on other areas such as communication." [1]

I'm not really convinced that I agree 100% with this article but I will say that if a larger company can take this initiative into practice with no solid results, they must still see the value of applying these practices. For a small company or home-based entrepreneur, I strongly feel that implementing these EI practices in your communication and business protocols will result in lower stress situations and give the business manager an upper hand in the way they view every day approaches to communication and personal conduct.

Regardless of what size your business is at this time, it will challenge you when you deal with difficult personalities and if you are not grounded in your beliefs and value as an entrepreneur, you can become very weakened and lose your self-esteem and passion for your business.

Another quote from an article that clearly states how powerful it is for an entrepreneur is taken from WHEN I WORK blog – "Up to 85% of our financial success is based on 'invisible skills' —traits like personality, how well we can communicate, and our ability to empathize, negotiate, and lead." It goes on to say, "According to Psychology Today, emotional intelligence is 'the ability to identify and manage your own emotions and the emotions of others.' In business (especially sales), this is often referred to as being good with people or having good people skills. But emotional intelligence isn't just about how well we interact with each other. It's also about how well we manage and interpret our own emotions." [2]

For me personally, I have gone through many stages of emotional intelligence in the way I have grown and developed my business over the last 5 years.

Here is my EI/EQ self-awareness path over the last 5 years as an entrepreneur:

YEAR 1 - I was struggling with a very low EI and as a result, I attracted a huge range of clientele. I had clients who were easy to work with and some very demanding and difficult who had low self-esteem. I was overly empathetic and took my own emotions and personal boundaries off the radar and put everyone else first, which led to me being burned out after my first year in business while working closely with over 50 international authors I helped publish.

YEAR 2 - I had started to learn more about EI, and it helped me to manage my communication a little more effectively with difficult clients. I found that the most difficult ones were struggling with low self-esteem and life had been hard on them, so as a result of them not processing their experiences, they were hard on others. I began to feel situations out and slowly started being more assertive with my boundaries.

YEAR 3 - At this time I had started developing my EI and I was learning how people would project their issues onto to me because they were conditioned by society to believe they could be demanding to me as my client or customer. I was not as confident in my body language because I kept myself closed off as I didn't want to offend but only please. I applied boundaries but was not sensitive enough and still felt uncomfortable because I was operating from a place of desperation and not a mindset of abundance.

YEAR 4 – By now, I had taken many more self-development courses over the years along with my own training and experiences from being an RN, working in health care for over 20 years. Walking the line as an entrepreneur was not easy and I personally struggled in the areas of empathy and compassion, which was like a never-ending battle of standing up for myself and taking care of other's needs first. I became more conscious of my personal space and how I wanted to represent myself. This new awareness permitted my hands to become freer to express myself once again because I was releasing so many emotional wounds that I had carried inside for years. Everything started coming together differently as I saw how effective communication, allowing support, and more resources coming around me released a lot of personal stress.

YEAR 5 - I am looking at life from a whole new perspective now and can appreciate the very thing I have promoted in my writing and coached my clients around for years, which is: you cannot change anyone who does not want to change themselves. You can only change yourself and the way that you see everything and everyone around you. I have no limitations in how I express myself now as an enlightened individual. I choose to stay grounded and use my essential oils to help me remain centered if I am in a situation that requires me to shift emotionally in an instant. By implementing an attitude of mindfulness and focusing on my business goals, I have completely restructured my entire business model for a more solid structure to serve my clients successfully which can be anywhere from 50 to 100 + people at any given time. I know that everyone has life issues. I can be supportive of my clients without feeling drained and compelled to fix their problems any longer. Instead I choose to empower and educate them to become leaders in their own right.

Everyone is responsible for themselves and just need to be shown the way they can own their behaviours and experiences for themselves. I feel this new approach of letting go of so much control has increased my confidence in myself, my clients, and everyone I interact with. This has strengthened all my business relationships, while releasing me of the burden to be everything for others. I use empathy on a daily basis, but I do not encourage low vibration behaviours. I choose to continually educate and get mentorship so I can be flexible in my perceptions and awareness of others.

EXCERCISE/ DISCUSSION QUESTIONS:

1. How have you worked with you clients over the year(s)?

   Make a list on a separate sheet of the years you have been in business and write out how your EI/EQ has evolved.

2. What areas do you feel need more clarity when working with your clients on an emotional level? Expand on any of the following or anything else you need addressing.

   Examples include:

   - Response to demands

     - Supporting clients who are needy and want more than was agreed

     - Keeping your boundaries clean and not washed out or grey

3. How do you categorize your emotional response or triggers?

4. How can you change the way you choose to express yourself now that you are aware of how you have been in the past?

5. Looking back, can you see what your body language was like in those past trigger experiences? How can you shift those behaviours now that you are aware?

6. When you are in various settings, do you notice if you struggle to gain attention or are aware of how to shift your communication style?

7. Do you communicate with empathy to your customers?

Thank you for taking the time to do this exercise to Strengthen the Weakened areas of your life. If you would like to work with me on creating a balance in your life and business, I would love to help you do so. Please contact me at lwlclienthelp@gmail.com

(1) http://hrpeople.monster.com/training/articles/2899-are-leaders-with-low-emotional-intelligence-weakening-your-bottom-line

(2) https://wheniwork.com/blog/why-emotional-intelligence-and-leadership-go-hand-in-hand/

Anita is the Brampton Chapter President of the Holistic Chamber of Commerce because she believes in supporting all entrepreneurs who work from a mind, body & spirit perspective. As a Registered Nurse with over twenty years in Health Care, she has worked with all age groups and diversities.

Anita has excellent written, and communication skills is empathetic and goal-oriented. She is as an ICF - Certified Professional Coach, Publisher, Law of Attraction Practitioner, and soon-to-be Master of NLP Practitioner, as well as a #1 and multiple Best-Selling author.

Email: **lwlclienthelp@gmail.com**

Website: **www.lwlpublishinghouse.com**

AFTERTHOUGHT

So now that you have read each of these Powerful, Inspirational Chapters, life-affirming messages and reviewed the solution-based stories written just for you, I am so blessed you found something just for you within these pages. It is our sincere wish that you find MORE healing in your life today. I trust you can now understand and appreciate how we were intent on making your healing become the center of our focus.

I want to encourage each of you to stretch and let go of your limitations my dear reader as you continue to ponder the wisdom and experiences of all these amazing authors. They have openly allowed you into their world of pain, heartache, hope, courage, strength, faith and victory to finding the healing in their own lives, so they can show you how to find your healing today.

As you can see, everyone within this beautiful book is accessible, and yes, they are real people just like you and me. Please feel free to reach out and connect with whomever you choose to if something you read within these pages resonated with you. I also encourage you to share your book or get one as a gift for someone you know needs encouragement and hope today.

The value that is within this book is priceless. Just like Gold never loses its value, the knowledge these lives poured into their Chapters is invaluable and worthy of review and application in one's daily life.

Now, my question to you is, what does your life look like? Are you struggling with keeping your life issues, trauma, grief an don't know how to help yourself then I encourage you to reach out to those close to you, a church leader, professional coach or counselor? You can talk to your family doctor if you are having a tough time coping with things. It is not always easy to keep it together whether it is a company, business or people and keep things running smoothly while building the life of your dreams.

I understand the frustrations, tears, and stress. I want to assist you in making your dreams and goals a reality.

If you would like more support, please speak to someone today instead of suffering another day silently alone. You matter, and you deserve to be living the best life possible.

Love, Peace & Abundance Blessings Always,

Anita Sechesky

#1 Best-Seller!

Originally published on October 24th, 2014. Our very first anthology became #1 and our revised edition with 23 MORE contributors became a best-seller once again. Own your copy now.

QR Code for orders

#Love - A New Generation of Hope Continues...

Compiled by Anita Sechesky, Foreword by Charlotte Howard

As the Compiler and Visionary of this book, it is my privilege to introduce you to the beautiful essence of love. It is my hope as you read the contributions from my thirty-nine co-authors, something will touch your heart within these pages. Our book will shift the way you view yourself, your loved ones and the world around you. Love begins within us. We all need love. When applied liberally in all areas of our lives, our perspectives begin to shift and the power of love's healing energy begins to flow.

Available worldwide where books are sold.
OR get your copy here: www.lwlpublishinghouse.com

QR Code
for orders

With everything that's happening in the world around you, get the book that simplifies the goals that every person wants to achieve. There's still something FIERCE in you that can MANIFEST the very life you desire!
This book will INSPIRE, EMPOWER, and ENLIGHTEN you to step into the life you've been yearning for.
If our International Visionaries can do it, so can you! We want to show you something that's extraordinary and unique to each individual. NOTHING is impossible if you believe in the power of your vision.

QR Code
for orders

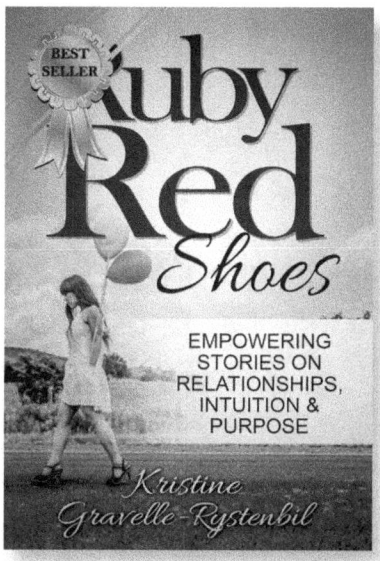

On the Ruby Red Shoes journey, every woman has a special message waiting to be heard by those who are ready for it. *Ruby Red Shoes: Empowering Stories on Relationship, Intuition & Purpose* is a coming together of heart-centered, inspired, and purpose-driven women to provide gentle guidance and insight to their soul sisters. In sharing of life wisdom through personal stories, each woman has an opportunity to meet a kindred spirit – one who gives her permission to shine and blossom on her journey of becoming the amazing woman she was born to be.

Available worldwide where books are sold.
OR get your copy here: www.lwlpublishinghouse.com

QR Code for orders

With so many self-help books out there, wouldn't it be nice to find one that shows how powerful the human mind, body and spirit are? Let us show you MORE healing stories and life affirming inspiration in our NEWEST revised edition. You will find courageous stories on the most devasting incidents and life experiences that many people face alone or with little support. As you read about our authors you may even find hope and recognize that there is MORE healing for you as well. The human heart is where we all connect as one.
This book can help Heal your World in so many ways!

QR Code for orders

The world is continually changing, but one hope remains the same - to be at peace in our daily lives. Our readers will understand that they are powerful enough to adapt a peaceful mindset. Everyone is capable of attracting a life of peace and prosperity. Read how thirty individuals from around the world established a life of peace and wellness, despite the struggles in their day-to-day lives.
As human beings, we have the ability to be at peace in any situation regardless of what's going on around us.

More Stories to Heal Your World Now

Available worldwide where books are sold.
OR get your copy here: www.lwlpublishinghouse.com

 QR Code for orders

As a professional clairvoyant and medium, I have always been directed by my Angelic guides. I have felt their beautiful light, experienced their unconditional love, and heard their uplifting messages which allowed me to help others find guidance and support. Fortunately, these Angelic beings are not exclusive to only intuitive people like myself! They are accessible to everyone and anyone who asks for their help and guidance.

"Guided by the Light – Following Your Angelic Guides" looks into the blessed energy that surrounds Angels, how they have touched us all in many ways, and how you can connect with your Angelic Guides.

QR Code for orders

When life changes right before our eyes, Hope is the one thing that remains when all else fails. What is it that keeps you in a place of peace and gratefulness? What do you do when no one understands or it feels like no one cares? The collective messages in this beautiful book will enlighten our readers to look beyond their present circumstances and find strength where they never looked before. Maybe it will inspire you to recognize the gifts of courage and inner peace from allowing something bigger than yourself to guide you to a place of certainty that cannot be put into words. Regardless of the circumstances, one thing remains...

Available worldwide where books are sold.
OR get your copy here: www.lwlpublishinghouse.com

QR Code for orders

H A L O: Lighting Up Heaven on Earth is a collection of stories written by an International Group of Heart and Service Centered Co-authors. We aim to connect with your heart to bless, inspire, uplift, empower, heal, and enlighten you with stories on Health, Abundance, Love, and more. It is our hope that by sharing our stories that the Soul Light within you awakens, expands, and radiates outwardly to touch the heart of all you encounter in beautiful ways.

QR Code for orders

Every woman deserves to feel accepted, loved, and treasured, much like a diamond is treated with Love, Joy, and Pride. Unfortunately, life doesn't always give us the desires of our hearts.So then it's up to us women to recognize the great and priceless value we possess within. The individual stories shared throughout this book will put that sparkle of hope back where it belongs... in your hands to wear proudly for the whole world to see who you really are!

More Stories to Heal Your World Now

Available worldwide where books are sold.
OR get your copy here: www.lwlpublishinghouse.com

 QR Code for orders

As the Publisher and Visionary of this new series of Multi-Vision books, it is my intention to bring more powerful self-healing and life-shifting stories to print. LWL PUBLISHING HOUSE promotes a living without limitations lifestyle. Let us create your legacy in print.

Stories of love. Love being the strongest energy in the Universe. These stories show us that if you are open to receive love, it can heal you through loss, birth, rebirth, and parts of us.

When life gives you lemons, do we always remember to make lemonade?

www.ingramcontent.com/pod-product-compliance
Lightning Source LLC
Chambersburg PA
CBHW070052080526
44586CB00013B/1026